TARLA DALAL *India's #1 Cookery Author*

Pregnancy
Cook Book

Your Complete
Food & Nutrition Guide

S&C
SANJAY & CO.
MUMBAI

Other Books By Tarla Dalal

INDIAN COOKING
Tava Cooking
Rotis & Subzis
Desi Khana
The Complete Gujarati Cook Book
Mithai
Chaat
Achaar aur Parathe
The Rajasthani Cookbook
Swadisht Subzian (New)

GENERAL COOKING
Exciting Vegetarian Cooking
Party Cooking
Microwave Cooking
Quick & Easy Cooking
Saatvik Khana
Mixer Cook Book
The Pleasures of Vegetarian Cooking
The Delights of Vegetarian Cooking
The Joys of Vegetarian Cooking
Cooking With Kids
Snacks Under 10 Minutes
Ice-Cream & Frozen Desserts
Desserts Under 10 Minutes (New)

WESTERN COOKING
The Complete Italian Cookbook
The Chocolate Cookbook
Eggless Desserts
Mocktails & Snacks
Soups & Salads
Mexican Cooking
Easy Gourmet Cooking
Thai Cooking
Chinese Cooking
Easy Chinese Cooking
Sizzlers & Barbeques (New)

TOTAL HEALTH
Low Calorie Healthy Cooking
Baby and Toddler Cookbook
Cooking with 1 Teaspoon of Oil
Home Remedies
Delicious Diabetic Recipes
Fast Foods Made Healthy
Healthy Soups & Salads (New)
Healthy Breakfast (New)

MINI SERIES
A new world of Idlis & Dosas
Cooking under 10 minutes
Pizzas and Pastas
Fun Food for Kids
Roz Ka Khana
Microwave - Desi Khana
T.V. Meals

Price Rs. 250/-

Published & Distributed by :

SANJAY & COMPANY
353/A-1, Shah & Nahar Industrial Estate,
Dhanraj Mill Compound, Lower Parel (W),
Mumbai - 400 013. INDIA.
Tel. : (91-22) 2496 8068
Fax : (91-22) 2496 5876
E-mail : sanjay@tarladalal.com

Recipe Research & Production Design
Pinky Dixit
Arati Fedane
Jyoti Jain
Ushma Negandhi

Printed by :
Jupiter Prints,
Mumbai

Food Stylist
Nitin Tandon

Nutritionists
Punam R. Desai
Nisha Katira

Photography
Vinay Mahidhar

Design
Satyamangal Rege

Illustrations
Ganesh Tayde

Pregnancy is one of the most wonderful periods in a woman's life. A time to look back with joy, be indulged beyond your wildest dreams, to look forward with barely suppressed excitement and a quiet certitude and faith in the powers above that all will be well.

A new life is being nurtured inside you, you will experience a host of different emotions and your mind will be filled with questions like "Am I eating enough?". "How can I make sure that my baby is being fed enough?". These are some of the questions that worry most mothers-to-be.

Gone are those days when old folks encouraged you to eat oily food so that you have an easy delivery or eat white coloured food for a fair complexioned child! These age-old beliefs are truly myths.

All that you eat before and during your pregnancy is largely responsible for not only your health, but your baby's too! This is why, right before you conceive till the time you are travelling through your pregnancy, you should eat a well-balanced healthy diet.

Live well and eat healthy, eat as much as you need and best of all eat food that you enjoy. Follow Mrs. Dalal for she whets your appetite, keeping your kilocalories in check, at the same time tantalizes your taste buds too!!

There is a difference between "Glowing with health" and "Growing with health" for both are poles apart. Let your baby do all the growing within your womb so that he/she is hale and hearty to enter this New World. You need to maintain your optimum body weight and nourish yourself with the right food.

Working with Mrs. Tarla Dalal proved to be a very enjoyable experience. She is one lady who wears her chef's cap with style and whips up the most delectable, innovative and nutritive recipes.

Long before you conceive, through and beyond the 9 months of your pregnancy, Mrs. Dalal has taken minute care to satisfy your palate. Meals, snacks to fit every occasion will be great treats and delights for you. This book will accordingly take care of every diet related need or question you might ever have.

We want this book to be your best friend. Someone you can turn to whenever a doubt arises and someone who can offer you a solution. This is a time for you and your baby. We want to ensure that this is a happy and memorable period.

But hey! Don't you forget that you are pregnant only for a while, so spread your wings and be free. Free like a bird to soar high into the sky and enjoy this high point in your life!!!

Anupadma

M.D. Obstetrician & Gynaecologist

Introduction

"It's time to be pampered,
And a time to be loved.
It's a time to eat right
And nourish every bite!!!"

The exaltation and pleasure you feel while being pregnant knows no bounds.

It's a roller coaster of emotions that you experience. Some of them being joy, contentment and nervousness coupled with tons of confusion. What to eat, when to exercise, how to relax, whom to consult are only some of the queries that can occur to you. This is but a natural state of mind of every pregnant woman. So don't vex yourself, as you are not alone in your confusion.

I'd like to share with you all the nutritional information on your diet during your pregnancy and also various home truths that my daughter-in-law and numerous young mothers shared with me. They were the ones who urged me to write this cookbook.

Once upon a time, joint families were the way to live. Grandmothers, mothers, mothers-in-law had all the remedies and provided all the answers to the expectant mother. But with today's changing family structure, the new mother no longer has this advantage. This book can be a helping hand for you when you are troubled. But most importantly, I hope it will calm you and provide you with solutions for your diet-related qualms and queries during this time.

Writing this book was a novel experience not only for me but for Dr. Dadina too. Working closely with Dr. Avan Dadina, a well-known gynaecologist and obstetrician who practices in Mumbai, we have specially compiled this book to meet the exceptional nutritional requirements of pregnant and lactating women. Dr. Dadina has generously shared with us her valuable time and her abundant experience for which I am deeply grateful. She has been practicing for a number of years and has taken care of many expectant mothers. With the guidance of a gynaecologist who has nurtured innumerable expectant mothers and their bouncing little babies, I guarantee that you are in good hands.

My team of nutritionists have carefully analysed each recipe to ensure that you get the correct combination of nutrients during each trimester.

The recipes in this book are for the various stages of your pregnancy keeping in mind your special nutritional requirements for each trimester starting from preconception right till the time of lactation. I've incorporated easy recipes that are quick to cook. They are healthy and invigorating and contain the minimal amount of ghee or oil. These recipes emulate the eating patterns of not only expectant mothers but are also great for your whole family long after you have delivered. As a result, this compact book is extremely handy and can be referred to almost any time during your pregnancy and long after your baby is born. But please keep in mind that no book, not even mine, can be a substitute for a good gynaecologist.

As Dr Avan said innumerable times during the making of this book, remember that, "You are only pregnant and are not a patient". So go ahead and enjoy these special 9 months.

I would also like to thank Dr. Pranav Pandya, (Bsc. MBBS, MRCOG, MD), who is a consultant in Fetal Medicine and Obstetrics at the University College London Hospital, U.K. He was kind enough to look at our text and to add some finer points.

Sit back, turn the pages, clarify your doubts and ease your worries away. After all, being pregnant is one of the greatest joys of all.............

Here's to celebrating a new life!!!!

Tarla Dalal

Index

Recipe Index

Juices and Drinks

Breakfast

Snacks

Dals and Vegetables

Rotis

Rice

Continental

Desserts

Pre-conception

Planning a Baby?

Everybody loves babies,
And for a woman, having a baby is like
making a dream come true.
So let this dream weave itself into reality.

The joy and excitement of bringing a new life into this world is not only pleasurable but also demands a lot of responsibility. You should be ready to accept it as a challenge by maintaining a healthy diet so as to nurture the new life growing within you.

A woman who is well nourished before conception begins her pregnancy with reserves of essential nutrients like protein, minerals (Iron and Calcium) and vitamins (Folic Acid, Vitamins A, C & E) to meet the needs of a growing fetus.

You might be apprehensive during your pregnancy, worrying that what you do and what you eat is not good enough. Well, let's put those thoughts aside and work at putting your fears to rest by looking after yourself and enjoying your pregnancy. Let us look forward to giving birth to a beautiful, healthy baby.

Here are a few things to keep in mind when you are planning to have a baby:

1. Maintain a weight that is appropriate for pregnancy as this is a better indicator of maternal health during your 9 months of gestation. Even if you are slightly overweight or underweight, there is no reason to panic as long as you are at a weight level that you are comfortable with. Here is a formula to help you determine what weight is appropriate for your height. Height (cm)- 105=Ideal Body Weight (kg.) (105 is a standard figure derived for women from Broca's index for ideal body weight.)
2. Do not smoke or drink alcohol or use any recreational drugs.
3. Select a gynaecologist and an obstetrician whom you trust and most importantly, feel comfortable with.
4. Have a complete medical checkup, including blood analysis which will indicate your iron, haemoglobin and folic acid status. These nutrients are vital during your pregnancy and are required in large quantities for the fetal growth and

development. It is important that you build up their reserves before you actually conceive.

Iron is essential for fetal blood formation, **Calcium** is necessary for the building of healthy bones and teeth and **Folic acid** is vital for the development of the fetal neural tubes during the first trimester. So eat foods that are rich in folic acid much before you conceive and throughout your pregnancy as it is one of the most needed vitamins required by your body during this time.
Keeping these requirements in mind, we have included recipes like Hariyali Dal (page 105) and Soya Upma (page 53) to nourish you as they are excellent sources of all these nutrients.

To find out more about foods that are rich in these four basic nutrients i.e. Calcium, Iron, Folic acid and Fibre, simply refer to the section at the end of the recipes (page 157 to 160) which lists out these foods along with their nutrient values.

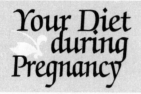
Your Diet during Pregnancy

Although the phrase "balanced diet" is so commonly used in our daily lives, very few of us actually know what it means. This is simply because we are unaware of what a balanced diet should comprise of.
I remember being absolutely at a loss for I did not know which food consumed by me had what dietary composition. It was only later that I understood the meaning of the term "balanced diet" which refers to eating a variety of foods chosen from each of the six major nutrient groups viz. protein, carbohydrates, fats, vitamins, minerals and water.

A balanced diet will also enable you to have an easy pregnancy that is free of complications like heartburn and free from digestive disorders like constipation, diarrhoea etc.

To assure a healthy pregnancy, you should supplement your diet with these major nutrients from the basic food groups mentioned below:

1. **Cereals** like wheat, jowar, bajra, ragi (nachni), rice etc.
2. **Pulses** like dals (moong dal, chana dal etc.)and legumes (matki etc.)
3. **Dairy** products like milk, pasteurized cheese, paneer, curds etc.

4. **Fruits** like banana, chickoo etc. and **Vegetables** like peas, pumpkin and green leafy vegetables like spinach, fenugreek etc.
5. **Fats** like ghee, oil, butter, sugar should be consumed in moderation.
   Have plenty of water and other fluids like juices, soups, buttermilk and milk shakes.

Now that you know exactly what a balanced diet should comprise of, here is a self-explanatory food guide, to know the various food groups and the quantities you can eat.

DAILY FOOD GUIDE DURING PREGNANCY			
FOOD GROUPS	No.of servings per day	What makes 1 Serving?	Suggested Recipes
CEREALS AND THEIR FLOURS Whole wheat, unpolished rice, jowar, bajra, ragi (nachni), bulgur wheat (dalia), corn, whole wheat pasta, whole wheat bread etc.	6 to 10 servings	1 slice of whole wheat bread (25 gm)* or 2 phulkas (30 gm)* or 1 chapati (25 gm)* or 1 paratha (25 gm)* or ½ cup all cooked cereals and pasta (60 to 80 gm)*	High Fibre Bread (page 71) Paushtic Roti (page 120) Bajra Khichdi (page 130) Easy Cheesy Vegetable Pasta (page 142)
PULSES **Whole** Moong, lobhia beans, rajma, chick peas (kabuli chana), etc. **Sprouts** Moong, rajma, matki etc. Masoor dal, chana dal, urad dal etc. **Flours** Moong dal flour, chana dal flour (besan)etc.	2 to 3 servings	¼ cup raw whole pulses (35 to 40 gm)* or ½ cup cooked whole pulses (70 to 80 gm)* or ½ cup sprouts (60 to 80 gm)* or ½ cup of raw or cooked dals (70 to 80 gm)* or ½ cup of flours (40 to 60 gm)*	Chick Pea Salad (page 98) Sprout and Fruit Bhel (page 70) Hariyali Dal (page 105) Moong Dal Dosa (page 54)

Daily food guide is continued on the next page...

FOOD GROUPS	No. of servings per day	What makes 1 Serving?	Suggested Recipes
VEGETABLES Carrot, beetroot, cucumber, brinjal, french beans, cluster beans (gavarfali), cauliflower etc. **Leafy Vegetables** Spinach (palak), fenugreek (methi), lettuce, radish leaves, coriander, cow pea (chawli) leaves, colocasia, cabbage etc.	3 to 5 servings	½ cup raw vegetables (50 to 70 gm)* or ½ cup cooked vegetables (50 to 70 gm)* or 1 cup raw leafy vegetables (15 gm of vegetables like mint, coriander, fenugreek and 40 to 60 gm of other leafy vegetables)* or ½ cup cooked leafy vegetables (15 gm of vegetables like mint, coriander, fenugreek and 40 to 60 gm of other leafy vegetables)*	Winter Vegetable Soup (page 89) Broccoli Aloo aur Paneer ki Subzi (page 107) Spinach Malfatti (page 138) Fruit and Lettuce Salad (page 100)
FRUIT Pineapple, sweet lime, orange, guava, watermelon, mango, apple etc. **Dried Fruits** Almonds, cashewnuts, walnuts, sesame seeds (til), peanuts, dates, figs, apricots etc.	2 to 3 servings	½ cup chopped fruits (50 to 60 gm)* or 1 big piece of fruit for e.g. melon wedge (100 to 130 gm)* or 1 cup fruit juice (200 ml)* or ¼ cup dried fruits (20 to 30 gm)*	Fruity Bean Salad (page 94) Pineapple Passion (page 47) Til Chikki (page 66) Fig and Apricot Shake (page 49)
DAIRY PRODUCTS Milk, curd, paneer, cheese etc.	2 to 3 servings	1 cup milk (200 ml)* or 1 cup curds (200 ml)* or ¼ cup chopped paneer (35 gm)* or ¼ cup shredded cheese (35 gm)*	Date and Banana Shake (page 46) Dahi Chane ki Subzi (page 108) Kalakand (page 150) Tossed Salad (page 99)
FATS AND SUGAR Ghee, oil, butter, sugar and jaggery	**	Although there is no specific recommendation for this group, approximately 2 tablespoons of fat and 2 to 3 teaspoons of refined sugar can be consumed per day.	Golpapdi (page 64) Cabbage Rice (page 131) Pineapple Crumble (page 146) Banana Walnut Pancakes (page 62)

* *The weights of all the foods mentioned in the above table are approximate.*
** *Fats should be consumed in moderation, as some foods like walnuts, sesame seeds and even cereals contain invisible fats which are also a part of our diet. Moreover excessive fat can also disturb the absorption of important nutrients like calcium in your body. Apart from making you put on weight.*

Recommended Dietary Allowance (RDA)

Wondering what RDA is all about? Well, it's the daily requirement of nutrients that your body needs as recommended by the Indian Council of Medical Research (ICMR). The Recommended Dietary Allowance (RDA), suggested for Indian women with a moderate activity level is given below along with an explanation of the functions and sources of all the major nutrients required during pregnancy.

Before conception, you should consume approximately 1900 to 2200 kcal/day. This is your daily energy requirement.

However, during pregnancy, your energy requirements are higher and you will need to consume between 2200 to 2500 kcal/day.

These requirements should be supplemented by a balanced combination of carbohydrates (cereals like whole wheat, ragi, jowar and parboiled rice), protein (pulses and legumes), vegetables (especially green leafy vegetables) and fat in moderation.

The keyword here is quality and not quantity. It's not about how much you eat, but what you eat.

1. All food groups provide energy, which is expressed in technical terms as kilocalories or what we commonly refer to as Calories. You require an adequate amount of energy to keep your strength up. You need to provide your body with 2200 to 2500 kcal of **Energy** per day.

2. **Protein** (65gm/day) in your maternal store is required for a good overall growth and development of your fetus.
   Good sources of protein are
   ✤ Pulses like moong dal, chana dal, matki etc.
   ✤ Dairy products (milk, pasteurized cheese, paneer, curds etc.)
   ✤ Soyabean and its products e.g. tofu and soya chunks are an excellent source of vegetarian protein.
   Try Subzi Dal (page 114) which is a very good example for this group.

3. **Calcium** (1000 mg/day) is required for the development of fetal bones and teeth. **So stock up by eating plenty of these foods**
   ✤ Dairy products (milk, pasteurized cheese, paneer, curds etc.)
   ✤ Soyabean and its products e.g tofu and soya chunks

✤ Dark green leafy vegetables like spinach, mint and fresh coriander etc.
✤ Til (sesame seeds) and ragi (nachni).
Try Paneer Palak Methi Rotis (page 123) which are a good combination of a dairy product and leafy vegetables and Kalaland (page 150) is loaded with calcium.

4. **Iron** (38mg/day) is an essential component of haemoglobin that supplies oxygen to each cell of the human body. In addition, it is required for the fetal red blood cell production. So do have iron in the required quantity or else you might become anaemic. Have no fear on that account for Mr. Iron's here!!

   Foods with high iron sources are
   ✤ Dried beans, peas and lentils
   ✤ Cereals and pulses
   ✤ Dried fruits like raisins, dates and figs
   ✤ Dark green leafy vegetables like spinach, mint, fresh coriander, cauliflower greens and vegetables like broccoli and pumpkin
   ✤ Til (sesame seeds), nuts (almonds, cashewnuts) and jaggery
   Try Usli (page 110) and Vegetable Stew (page 143). Do not forget tempting dhoklas made of Methi and Palak (page 56) to enrich your iron stores.

5. **Folic acid** (400 mcg/day) is an essential vitamin required almost 12 weeks before you conceive and also during the first trimester for the growth and development of the brain and spine of the fetus. Folic acid is also required throughout the pregnancy for the formation of blood. Its deficiency leads to anaemia in the mother.

   Raise your folic acid levels by enjoying
   ✤ Potatoes eaten with their skin on (i.e. unpeeled). Be sure to scrub the peel very clean.
   ✤ Vegetables like cluster beans (gavarfali), spinach, peas, broccoli, beetroot and ladies fingers
   ✤ Cereals and pulses
   ✤ Soyabean and its products e.g. tofu and soya chunks
   ✤ Nuts (almonds, cashewnuts and walnuts) and sesame seeds (til)
   Try Soya Mutter ki Subzi (page 106) which is a good storehouse of this vitamin.

6. **Fat** is a concentrated source of energy and a daily requirement of 30 gm/day is essential. The fat that accumulates throughout your pregnancy acts as an energy reserve. When the supply of kilocalories is inadequate, the accumulated fat is used to support the needs of your rapidly growing fetus.

7. **Vitamin C** (40 mg/day) is imperative to make yourself immune against infections and diseases. It is also required for the formation of collagen which is a protein that provides structure to the bones, cartilage, muscles and blood vessels.
    Boost your vitamin C levels with
    ✤ Citrus fruits like oranges, sweet lime and lemon
    ✤ Amla
    ✤ Vegetables like cabbage, coriander leaves and capsicum
    Try Fruity Bean Salad (page 94) which will nourish you with plenty of vitamin C and add that zing you need.

8. **Vitamin A** (Beta-Carotene 2400 mcg/day) is required for clear vision, healthy skin and immunity for both you and your baby. Excessive vitamin A can however lead to toxicity and can be harmful. It is usually not necessary to supplement your diet with any other form of vitamin A (e.g. in tablet form), if you consume the following natural food sources mentioned below.
    Maintain your vitamin A levels with
    ✤ Yellow orange vegetables like carrot and pumpkin
    ✤ Fruits like mango, papaya and tomatoes
    ✤ Dark green leafy vegetables like spinach, mint and fenugreek
    ✤ Whole milk
    Try Carrot Pancakes (page 145) which will provide you plenty of vitamin A.

9. **Vitamin D** is synthesized through sunlight which aids the absorption of calcium in the body. Hence, there is no dietary recommendation for this nutrient in our tropical climate.

10. In comparison to non-vegetarian foods, vegetarian diets are deficient in **Vitamin B12**. But don't let that hamper your spirits as soya milk and soya products in particular provide an appreciable amount of this vitamin. Try Soya Upma (page 53) which will perk up your vitamin B12 levels.

11. **Iodine** is one of the major important minerals which is required for your baby's brain development. To maintain adequate iodine levels in your body, use iodised salt in your daily cooking.
   You can also get iodine from the natural sources like
   ✤ Cereals (rice, wheat, jowar etc.)
   ✤ Nuts and oilseeds (til etc.)

The Fresh Feast
(Cooking Right)

"Pick and choose all you want,
Don't freeze if you please,
Fresh vegetables is the way,
Boil, steam and sauté,
So why not eat it every day."

Now that you are more acquainted with the nutrients you require, it will be beneficial for you to follow these few tips to preserve the nutrients present in the food during the cooking process and also while buying, handling and storing.

1. Buy only the freshest fruits and vegetables available in the market. Seasonal fruits are the most nutritious as they ripen without the usage of additional chemicals and are more reasonably priced.
2. Refrigerating food for long periods results in the loss of vital nutrients. So buy in small quantities and cook for the day!
3. As far as possible, eat vegetables and fruits unpeeled so that your body receives the right amount of fibre and nutrients. Vegetables and fruits like cucumber, potatoes and carrots have vital nutrients right under the peel which we lose out on if we peel them. Remember to scrub these vegetables thoroughly before you eat them as they may contain a thin film of mud and pesticides. However, scrub tough skinned vegetables whose skins are inedible like turnips or yam (suran) thoroughly and then gently scrape a thin layer off using a knife or a peeler.
4. Soaking vegetables in water for a longer period of time will make them lose many valuable, water-soluble vitamins like vitamin B and C.

5. Vegetables should be cooked carefully so that they retain most of their nutrients during the cooking process. Therefore, it is better to sauté or steam vegetables rather than to boil them. If you do boil the vegetables, use the minimum quantity of water and cook only until the vegetables become tender. Whenever possible, cook food in large pieces as vegetables cut into small pieces lose more nutrients. Preferably, cover your foods while cooking to preserve the volatile nutrients that are present in vegetables and fruits.

6. Preparing a fresh salad or raita just before meals is the best habit to adopt. Squeezing lemon on salads is great as it contains vitamin C which helps in the absorption of iron from your meal. Eat salads like Energy Salad (page 93) and Tossed Salad (page 99) since they will surely refresh you.

7. Do include a large amount of sprouts in your diet as sprouting aids in easy digestion. Sprouting destroys the anti nutritional factors like phytates that are present in all legumes. They are called anti nutritional factors because they hamper the absorption of vital nutrients like iron and calcium from your food. These complex substances (phytates) are broken down to simpler forms when you sprout them, making them easier to digest. Sprouted legumes have higher vitamin C, iron and calcium levels than those that are not sprouted. Sprouted chick peas (kabuli chana) and sprouted green gram (moong) are excellent sources of vitamin C. So here's to happy sprouting!! Try Sprout and Fruit Bhel (page 70) or Sprout Pulao (page 134).

8. Avoid using soda bi-carbonate while cooking as it destroys most of the essential nutrients present in the food.

First Trimester

The first three months of pregnancy are called the "first trimester". During this trimester, you will show only a few outward signs that you are pregnant. Nonetheless, you will experience tremendous physical and emotional changes which are new and also exciting.

Throughout pregnancy, your baby needs a ready supply of energy and a high quality of nutrients for its growth. It is during the first few weeks after conception that the fetus begins to form the organs and the heartbeat can be detected by the second month. However, growth and maturation continues right till the end of your pregnancy (gestation).

Your state of mind during your pregnancy will also affect your baby. Read books that you enjoy, listen to music and do all the things that makes you happy and relaxed. Some women find cooking or baking relaxing, while others enjoy gardening or reading.

As the months roll by, you may get exhausted quickly. Overcome your tiredness by taking short naps whenever you feel the need to without feeling guilty. Also allow your loved ones to fuss over you and pamper yourself too! Enjoy all the attention you receive, especially from your husband. Ask your husband to rub your back and shoulders as a light massage on the back muscles can also be a stress reliever.

Try and enjoy every split second of your pregnancy for it is filled with delight, euphoria, anxiousness and apprehension too! As you travel through the following trimesters, you might experience some discomforts, but every pregnancy has its ups and downs and these are changes that happen in different degrees to most pregnant women. So read on to find ways to ease these situations...

Dealing with Morning Sickness (Nausea/Vomiting)

You might feel faint and want to throw up repetitively.

This is but a normal feeling, so don't get perturbed. With every passing day, your body experiences changes which may cause you nausea, that may or may not be accompanied by vomiting. This usually lasts through the first trimester and then eases out by the second trimester. Some lucky women don't experience this phase at all.

Nausea occurs most commonly in the early half of the day and thus it gets the name "morning sickness". However, you can feel nauseous at any time of the day or night.

Some of you may find it more difficult to cope with nausea than others.
If you're only feeling nauseous and are not vomiting, try chewing on mint, cardamom or clove to make you feel better. You can also try keeping Golpapdi (page...) in your mouth to help relieve your nausea. It will also nourish you at the same time. Sucking on ginger or lemon is another alternative to keep your nausea at bay. Avoid chewing on betel nut (supari) and other packaged mouth fresheners.

You may worry that your baby will not receive proper nourishment if you're vomiting or are nauseous and are not able to eat well. Put these fears to rest as your baby will still continue to get sufficient nourishment from your reserves. **This is one of the reasons why gynaecologists recommend that you stock up on essential nutrients much before you conceive.**

Try and keep yourself busy, as the lesser you think about it, the less it will bother you. To calm these uneasy days, these are a few things to keep in mind:

1. Eat low fat foods that are rich in carbohydrates like toast, khakhra or chikki etc. These foods will help relieve the sensation of morning sickness. Turn the pages and try out Whole Wheat Methi Khakhras (page 65), Bajra Khakhras (page 68), Til Chikki (page 66) etc. These are mildly flavoured foods lacking in strong smells which will not aggravate the nausea and will calm you. If you can manage it, have a bowl of cereal with milk for it's a great way to start your day.
2. Have a mid-morning snack consisting of a yoghurt shake, fruit juice, dried fruits like dates, apricots [have them whole or in the form of shakes like Fig and Apricot Shake (page 49)] or just any fruits that you like.
3. Avoid eating foods with excessive seasoning and also those which are strongly flavoured as they can aggravate nausea. You can have mildly

flavoured dishes like Cucumber Curd Rice (page 132) to help relieve you.

4. If you are vomiting, you may continue to lose a lot of fluids along with the nutrients. Try and consume at least 2 litres of fluid every day. You can have these fluids in any form suitable to you, preferably milk shakes, buttermilk, juices, soups and water.

5. Sipping cold water, juices or shakes from time to time will keep nausea at bay and will also ensure that you get your fluid requirement for the day. Sip on sherbets or drinks like My Fair Lady (page 50) etc.

6. Apart from hormonal changes, nausea is sometimes related to stress and anxiety. Deep breathing or listening to soothing music calms the mind and reduces stress. Learn to slowly breathe and relax whenever you experience stress. Meditation and yoga are also helpful for relaxation. The more relaxed you are, the easier it will be for you to cope with this discomfort.

7. Avoid self-medication. If your morning sickness persists for several weeks, do consult your gynaecologist as she may be able to prescribe some medication to ease your discomfort.

 ## Second Trimester

With the onset of the second trimester, you are almost half way through your pregnancy. This trimester is a time of pleasant changes for you and your baby as it is a period of rapid growth and development of the fetus.
During this time, the fetus can move, kick and even hear your voice.

You will stop feeling sick and will be able to enjoy your pregnancy during this trimester. You won't be "huge" as yet and will feel on the top of the world.

Your appetite will get better as your morning sickness will soon begin to disappear. This is also the time you may crave to eat spicy dishes, sour foods or even sweets. Dosa, Idli, Mexican Rice, Tomato Soup... may be some of the foods you may keep craving for. Enjoy the foods you long to eat, but eat them in moderation. Don't binge on pickles and spicy foods. You need to increase your energy and protein levels by eating a healthy nutritious diet. Have Spinach Malfatti (page 138) for a nourishing and delicious meal.

Remember to include iodine in your diet as it is essential for your baby's growth during this trimester. The best way to ensure this is to use a good quality brand of iodised salt in your daily cooking.

Despite being extra cautious about all that you eat, you may face digestive disorders like loose motions and constipation. These are but normal changes that can occur during your pregnancy. Both constipation and diahrroea are relieved by the same natural cure i.e. adding fibre to your diet. Paradoxically, fibre binds the stools during loose motions and flushes the system in case of constipation by adding bulk. Have plenty of fruits, vegetables, buckwheat, dates, prunes, apricots and dried figs as these foods are rich in fibre and loaded with nutrients too.

During this trimester, you may also feel the urge to urinate more frequently. This is because your uterus is enlarging and thus compresses the urinary bladder. It is a natural change that will occur as a result of which you will have to answer nature's calls more frequently, which will deplete your body fluids. Drink at least 2 litres of fluid every day to supplement this loss of fluids.
Relieve yourself as often as you feel the urge to, so that you do not burden your bladder. Many a times, you may tend to drink less water so as not to visit the toilet frequently. But remember that drinking less water won't help you and could cause you more discomfort. It may even cause water retention (oedema) as all the toxins present in your body will not be flushed out.
Leg cramps can also occur during this trimester, primarily because of over-exertion or deficiency of calcium in your diet. Dairy products as well as green leafy vegetables will provide you with plenty of calcium. Try and include a combination of these foods in your daily diet.
Do remember to visit your gynaecologist more frequently this trimester onwards, as you do need to be monitored more carefully now.

❧ Oedema (Swelling)

Oedema is swelling which develops during the second trimester as a result of water retention. It can occur on any part of your body but for most pregnant women, it is more predominant on the feet, hands and the face. Despite the water retention, do make sure you continue your regular intake of water and fluids. Water is a natural diuretic, which helps to flush out all the toxins that cause water retention in your body, while cleansing your system too. Water is not the cause of oedema (water retention). In fact it is the cure!

Salt is one of the major culprits which aggravates oedema. Do try to avoid papads, pickles, salted snacks like wafers and processed and preserved foods as they have a high salt content which can cause water retention.

You don't have to cut down your salt intake drastically, especially without consulting your gynaecologist or nutritionist, as you should be consuming at least ½ teaspoon of salt every day to maintain optimal electrolyte balance in your blood (i.e. the sodium and potassium balance).

Don't take any diuretic tablets to relieve you. These will only make the kidneys produce more urine and in the process will deplete your body fluids. These tablets are not advised as they may be harmful to both you and your baby. Instead, include fruits like papaya and pineapple which have natural diuretic properties and will help you cope with not only oedema but also constipation. So indulge in the delicious Pineapple Passion (page 47).

If you are feeling uncomfortably puffy due to water retention, enjoy all the fruity shakes and fresh salads for 1 day and try to avoid any cooked foods. This will have a natural dieuretic effect, flushing out the unnecessary water retention.

Coping with Heartburn (Acidity)

Acidity or heartburn is another source of discomfort for some pregnant women. It can make you feel uneasy with a burning sensation in your chest, or make you nauseous if it is really severe. Some women have acidity much before they conceive, while some develop it only during their pregnancy.

You might feel the urge to rely on antacids when what you actually need is plenty of water, a good nutritious diet and a relaxed mind, free from the hustle and bustle of daily life. Get plenty of fresh air, exercise and a stress free environment. Work on soothing your body and mind for this is the best medication you can prescribe yourself. In this matter, YOU are your best doctor!! I know all of this is easier said than done.

To ease heartburn, follow these tips and you will sail through the third trimester...

1. Have 3 to 4 glasses of buttermilk every day if you can handle it as it is God's nectar for acidity. You can even have fruity variations like My Fair Lady (page 50) and Strawberry Chickoo Shake (page 51).
2. Try eating 4 to 5 smaller meals during the day, instead of eating 2 to 3 large meals. Some of these small meals can be a khichdi like Wholesome Khichdi (page 136) or Date and Banana Shake (page 46). Combinations like these will satiate you and at the same time will provide you with good nourishment.
3. Eat your evening meal at least an hour or two before you go to bed. Try and stay upright after you have eaten, take a small walk or prop yourself up with pillows for a while. This prevents the reversal of food from the stomach with additional digestive acids that result in heartburn.
4. Eating your meals in a calm, pleasant and serene atmosphere helps. Avoid spicy and oily foods as these will tend to make you feel uncomfortable.
5. Drink more water (at least 6 to 8 glasses in a day) and increase your intake of fruit juices, soups and milk shakes. Consume at least 2 litres of fluid every day. Supplement your fluid intake with Guava Drink (page 48), Golden Broth (page 87) etc.

6. For some, acidity arises because of citrus fruits or their juices. If this occurs with you, avoid such fruits. Stay on non-acidic fruits like melons, bananas, chickoos etc.

Exercise

Slow but steady is the way to go!!
Your activities may seem a little slower as you will tend to get exhausted more quickly, but do remember that exercise is beneficial during your pregnancy. It will tone your muscles and keep you agile enough to have an easier labour. The best form of exercise is the one you have been comfortable with in the past. But consult your gynaecologist before you indulge in any form of rigorous exercise.

A good exercise program can give you the strength and endurance you'll need to carry the weight you gain during pregnancy and to handle the physical stress of labour. Plus it will make getting back into shape much easier after the baby is born. Exercise is also a great way to beat the pregnancy blues; a recent study found that staying active can boost your level of serotonin, a brain chemical linked to mood.

Even your regular household chores are a good form of exercise, but do not over-exert or strain yourself doing chores that are strenuous to perform. There's nothing like taking a walk with the fresh air blowing on your face. An early morning walk is recommended as this is the best time to synthesise vitamin D in your body from the early morning sunlight.
Vitamin D helps in the absorption of calcium which is an essential nutrient required throughout your pregnancy.

The key to exercising correctly is to continue only till you reach just below the point of exhaustion without exerting yourself unnecessarily. Some women may be able to walk for an hour without getting tired whereas others might get tired in 30 minutes.

Yoga and swimming are also excellent forms of exercise that can be continued well into your third trimester. The more active you are during this period, the easier it will be for you when you deliver. Research shows that women who have had an active pregnancy have a much better chance of having a normal delivery.

Third Trimester
Preparing for Labour

The countdown has begun...
These last three months are very crucial for you and your baby. All major growth and maturation of the organs is being completed during this time. It is during this trimester that you prepare yourself for childbirth and lactation.
During this time, your baby is reaching its optimal growth and weight. It is probably too big to move around but nonetheless can kick strongly and can slide slowly in the womb. Now that your tummy has grown larger, you might be a tinge uncomfortable. Sleeping on your back is one of the common problems you might face as it puts a lot of weight on your spine and the blood circulation will get slower which can adversely affect your baby. Sleep on your side using a pillow to support your back or prop your back up with pillows while lying down. You should eat well and rest enough to prepare for labour.

Physical and mental relaxation is a must during this phase of your pregnancy so that you are prepared to face the changes that will arise with the arrival of your baby.

Also, remember to continue your walking or yoga as they will prove to be helpful during your labour. Exercising regularly helps in toning your muscles, thus making your delivery an easier one. Do consult your doctor, however, as each pregnancy is unique and has its own requirements during this period depending on your health.

Now that you eagerly await the arrival of your baby, it is imperative that you stock up on all the important nutrients that are required for you and your little one.

Eating Right

During this trimester, your diet should provide adequate nutrients to your body so that it is prepared to cope with the additional requirements to nourish your baby after birth.

During this trimester, your baby will have become large, leaving little room in your mid section for food and you may lose your appetite in similar ways to the way you did in the first trimester. Eat foods that are light enough to keep you from feeling uncomfortable but are packed with nutrients. Try Wholesome Khichdi (page 136), Paneer Palak Methi Roti (page 123) or Bean Soup (page 88). Have small frequent meals that are not spicy or oily as the latter will upset you.

Weight gain is also very crucial as your body gets ready for lactation. The foods you select should have a good combination of nutrients to support your pregnancy and prepare you for lactation.

Avoid any rigid timing for your meals. Eat at any time of the day but choose your food wisely considering the nutritional value. Fruits, salads and fluids are most important. Milk shakes and lassi too are great refreshers. During your last trimester, try to incorporate garlic, methi, garden cress (subza) seeds, milk and almonds in your daily diet. These foods are also called as galactogogue foods i.e. they stimulate the production of breast milk.

The additional requirement for iron, calcium and fibre continues.

Iron

A high level of iron is crucial throughout your pregnancy especially during labour. The fetus also requires iron to build up its stores before birth. If the maternal stores of iron during these nine months of pregnancy are adequate, then the fetal requirements are also fulfilled. But these fetal stores last for only four months after delivery. Therefore, the necessity for weaning (introducing new foods in your baby's diet) arises after the fourth month of delivery. Recipes like Paatal Bhaji (page 112) will help you to supplement the iron stores in your diet.

Calcium

You must increase your intake of calcium. It is beneficial for breast milk and is required for the development of baby's bones and teeth. Leg cramps can occur due to calcium deficiency. Calcium sources can be combined with other food groups to make a tasty dish like Easy Cheesy Vegetable Pasta (page 142).

Fibre

Fibre in your diet will help in relieving constipation problems. Try to consume natural and unprocessed foods like fruits, green leafy vegetables and whole wheat products, as they are rich in fibre. Guava is one of the best sources of fibre. Do not ignore this humble fruit, as it can help to get rid of your constipation problems.

Zinc

This mineral is essential for your baby's growth and development and you can get your daily requirement by the regular consumption of cereals, pulses and greens such as spinach and broccoli.

Fluids

You should consume at least 2 litres of water daily especially if you are prone to water retention. In addition to water, you can supplement your diet with fruit juices, soups, milk shakes, buttermilk and coconut water as they are rich in nutrients and will provide you with instant energy!

Pregnancy Weight Gain Recommendations

You will be a tinge overweight on the scale, and for once, you won't feel guilty about those extra pounds. This time you will actually enjoy putting them on.
Gaining weight is an essential part of pregnancy.

Yes, you will gain weight and you have to, but how much and during which trimester may still be a mystery to you. All women do not gain the same amount of weight during pregnancy. This is because of differences in height, weight, physical activity and metabolism. Women who are underweight at the start of a pregnancy need to gain more weight as compared to women who are overweight.

There is no chart that says you have to put on "x" amount of weight after so many weeks. Most mums-to-be worry that if they do not put on the recommended amount of weight, their baby will not be healthy. It's a myth that the more weight you put on during your pregnancy, the healthier your baby will be. However, the overall average weight gain during your pregnancy should be 10 to 12 kg.

During the first trimester (0 to 3 months), you may put on 1 to 2 kilograms (kg.). Or ironically, instead of putting on weight, you may actually lose upto 2 kg. as a result of morning sickness (nausea and vomiting). Do not get anxious about the weight loss and try and eat small meals throughout the day to keep your strength up. Drink plenty of fluids to substitute the loss of fluids that takes place if you are vomiting. Your baby will be nourished with all the nutrients you will have accumulated before conception.

During the second trimester (4 to 6 months), most women usually put on about 1 to 2 kg. per month and during the third trimester (7 to 9 months), the weight gain can be about 2 to 3 kg. per month as your baby is now growing rapidly.

Less than half of the total weight you will gain resides in the fetus, placenta, and amniotic fluid; the remainder is accumulated in the breast tissues, fluid, blood and maternal stores, which is largely composed of body fat. This is where you will draw your resources from when breast feeding.

To keep up your resources, eat plenty of dals, pulses, vegetables and fruits during this time. Try and eat oily, sugary foods and chocolates in moderation as these provide empty calories and will only make you feel uneasy.

There is a difference however between "Glowing with Health" and "Growing with Health".

The kind of food you consume during your pregnancy will determine how much weight you will put on. Stay off the ghee-laden mithai and junk food and nourish yourself with the high fibre foods, as these are imperative for you at this time. Quality is far more important than quantity. Have healthy foods that will nurture you and your baby. Let your baby do all the growing within you. Keep in mind that it is a time solely for you to nourish your baby, so eat wisely. If you crave for sweets, choose dates or fruits over mithai and pastries. "But is ok to binge once in a while", says Dr. Dadina.

Snacking between Meals

Keep your worries at bay,
as you snack on food all day,
for a very pregnant you,
this is exactly what you should do.

After the first trimester, you may no longer be able to consume 2 to 3 large meals as you used to. Try and have small and frequent meals throughout the day as large meals may cause heartburn and nausea. Remember to include at least four of the basic food groups like cereals, pulses, vegetables and fats when you're snacking. For example, you can have Thalipeeth (page 73), Sprout and Fruit Bhel (page 70) etc.

Snacking through the day is vital but think before you reach for your favourite snack foods so that you fulfil your craving for salt, sweet and spices in a sensible way. Here are a few guidelines about how to go snacking.......

Include more fruits and salads as snacks to add fibre to your diet. Try to include fruits in different forms like Fruit and Lettuce Salad (page 100) or Date and Banana Shake (page 46). Avoid deep fried foods and fatty foods like pakodas, mithai, pastries etc. Banana Walnut Pancakes (page 62) are a better alternative for a snack rather than fried or sugary foods.

32

Avoid drinking tea or coffee with your snacks. Instead, have a fruit juice or a milk shake. Tea or coffee hinders the absorption of iron from your food due to the presence of tannins. Have herbal tea or decaffeinated tea or coffee because these are healthier options.

Select snacks that are low in kilocalories but are nutritionally adequate. Aerated waters should be consumed in moderation. These drinks contain empty kilocalories which only help to put on weight but have no nutritive value. Instead, have Pineapple Passion (page 47) or Guava Drink (page 48).

Avoid salty snacks like wafers, popcorn, cheese balls etc. If you still crave for these foods, then eat them in moderation and combine them with a healthier snack like fruits or upma, poha or cookies that are made of whole wheat flour so that you pamper your tastebuds and fulfil your nutrient requirements. Flip the pages and try Chocolate Chip and Oatmeal Cookies (page 69) or Mooli Muthias (page 74).

Select foods with minimum preservatives as some preservatives can have an adverse effect on the fetus. Read the labels mentioned on the food packages very carefully. They will tell you more about the nutrients they contain.
Preferably eat homemade food as you can be assured of its nutritional quality.

If you do snack out, make sure you choose your snack carefully. Eat well-heated foods when eating outdoors. If you're eating a dosa, try and avoid the chutney as it is usually at a temperature that can harbour germs very quickly. Avoid eating raw foods like salads and also street side snack foods as the microbial content of these foods may be high and could make you ill.

....

Eating Out

Nine months is a very long time to eat "ghar ka khana." Homemade food can get monotonous after a while and dining out can be an enjoyable change for you during your pregnancy.

It doesn't matter whether you are lunching at the Oberoi or enjoying a sumptuous dosa from your favourite dosa vendor just around the corner (remember not to have the chutney, though). Do indulge yourself, but the key is in "moderation".

You might crave to eat a particular dish at your favourite restaurant or snack on a bag of wafers. Munch on a few wafers if you must and then follow it up with a fruit or a milk shake so that you receive the nutrients your body craves for.

Most restaurant dinners tend to start off late and you may be really hungry by then, with the result that you may end up bingeing on fried starters or calorie-laden food. To avoid this, if you're anticipating a late dinner, have a small snack or a piece of fruit before you leave home.

When you're eating out, select foods that are low in fat and sugar. Choose a fruit juice or a lassi instead of carbonated beverages.

Have a wholesome soup with plenty of vegetables or a salad with a low fat dressing. Dress your salad with a very small quantity of mayonnaise. Ask your server/waiter to bring the dressing on the side. It's the oil-laden dressings that make salads unhealthy. If you are having salad, ensure it is freshly prepared for you since salad that is kept for long can cause you a lot of discomfort, as raw foods harbour bacteria very quickly. Include a raita if you don't want to eat just greens for your salad. This will also supplement your calcium intake.

Choose a whole wheat paratha or roti instead of white bread or naan made out of maida. Maida is refined flour which provides no real nutrition and will only lead to weight gain.

Have vegetables along with plenty of pulses and dals and ask your server or waiter to use less oil, butter and cream in cooking your meal.

Try and avoid fried items and desserts. If you really crave for desserts, select a less fatty, fruit based dessert and share it with someone, so that you don't feel obligated to finish the entire portion.

Don't feel guilty if you can't do justice to your food. Wastage is better than overeating. Most often when we eat out, we tend to overeat because we do not want to waste the food we have ordered. Pack the left overs so you can relish them later when you're hungry or you can give it to someone on your way home.

PostPartum and Lactation

Congratulations!!!
You're now a mummy!!

Labour will leave you with a lot of mixed emotions It will leave you contented, blissful and exhausted. It can be a long and tiring process for some moms, while some might have it really easy. Once your little one arrives, your entire world will be bustling and bubbling with effervescence, exuberance and joy. It will be a time for you to shower your baby with unconditional love.

The period after delivery/ labour is called post partum and lactation. The term lactation means secretion of milk by the mammary glands (breasts). During the first few days after birth, a cloudy fluid called colostrum will be secreted in place of milk. This fluid is very beneficial for your baby as it contains important antibodies to protect your little one from infections and diseases. Colostrum provides adequate nutrition to the infant until the appearance of true milk, 2 or 3 days after delivery. Breast feeding is very important as it helps to build a strong bond between you and your baby, and is also the best form of nourishment for your newborn infant.

There is no need to panic if you do not produce a lot of milk to feed your baby immediately after you deliver. It will gradually increase as you start feeding your baby more frequently. Your state of mind along with your diet influences the quantity of milk you produce. The more relaxed you are, the more milk you will produce.

The quantity and quality of milk produced is in no way related to the size of your breast but is dependent on the amount of fluids you consume. So drink plenty of juices, milk shakes, buttermilk, soups, water etc. Have at least 4 litres of fluid per day. The amount of milk produced also depends on the frequency at which your baby feeds.
The more often your baby feeds, the more milk will be produced. If you don't breast feed often, the milk won't be produced efficiently. This is nature's way of adapting to new changes. Let your feeding be guided by the baby's hunger pangs. Don't fix any rigid timing to feed your little one. Your baby will let you know when he's hungry by crying out for you.

Breast Feeding and its importance

Breast feeding your little one is one of the most invaluable gifts God has bestowed upon you. Grannys, mothers, gynaecologists and paediatricians today encourage breast feeding. Breast milk is a natural, pure and unadulterated form of nourishment and is a must for your young one. It provides antibodies to your baby which is why it is superior to formula feeds or cow's milk. So breast feeding your baby is one of the wisest decisions you can make. Read beyond this to know the goodness of mother's milk.............

1. Breast feeding is an experience that nurtures the emotional bonding between the mother and child. The feeding position will make your baby feel "safe" as the physical closeness will be similar to that it had in your womb for 9 months during gestation.

2. It is a very convenient way to feed your baby at any place and time.

3. A breast fed baby does not require any vitamin supplements as breast milk fulfils all the child's requirements. The nutritional quality of breast milk is much higher than that of cow's milk or buffalo's milk as it contains more lactose (milk sugar), more vitamins A, C and E than cow's milk or buffalo's milk. Fat and iron present in breast milk is better absorbed than the iron in cow's milk.

4. Fat and protein in the breast milk are more easily digested, which is why the danger of gastro-intestinal problems is low in breast fed newborn babies.

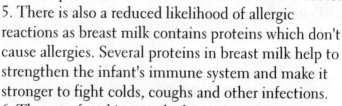

5. There is also a reduced likelihood of allergic reactions as breast milk contains proteins which don't cause allergies. Several proteins in breast milk help to strengthen the infant's immune system and make it stronger to fight colds, coughs and other infections.

6. The act of sucking on the breast promotes development of the jaw and facial muscles of your baby.

While you're breast feeding, you will require a lot more calories than you did during your pregnancy. This is because breast feeding your baby will make you burn 3500 kcal per day. However you need to consume only 2400 to 2700 kcal per day during the first 6 months of lactation, if you are exclusively breast feeding your baby. You may wonder where all the extra calories are going to come from; this is when you will start to burn up all the maternal stores that were accumulated during your pregnancy in preparation for lactation. It's nature's way of letting you get back in shape naturally. Stay off the ghee laden post partum dishes and feast on a balanced diet while also ensuring that you have at least 4 litres of fluid every day.

Most doctors recommend that you breast feed for 1 year. Out of this period, your baby should exclusively be breast fed for 4 to 6 months and then you can gradually start weaning by slowly introducing your baby to a variety of foods so that it is no longer completely dependent on you at the end of one year. (*For weaning recipes for your tiny bundle, look out for my Baby and Toddler Cookbook.)

During the last 6 months of lactation, your energy requirements will decrease to about 2250 to 2550 kcal per day as you will now begin to wean your little one gradually.

1. **Protein** requirements during the first 6 months of lactation are 75 gm/day. During the last 6 months of lactation, the protein requirements change to 68 gm/day.
    A good combination of cereals and pulses along with vegetables like that given in the recipe of Wholesome Khichdi (page 136) includes rice (cereal), moong dal (pulse) and vegetables (lauki and carrot).

2. **Fat** is a concentrated source of energy and 45 gm/day of it is required while you're lactating. Fat is required in moderation to supplement your maternal stores to ensure optimal secretion of breast milk.

3. **Calcium** (1000 mg/day) is required for the baby's development of bones. Breast milk is a great source of calcium and depriving yourself of calcium won't change the calcium levels in your breast milk. But in that case,

unfortunately the breast milk will draw its calcium from your bones making you more susceptible to Osteoporosis later in life.

4. **Iron** (30 mg/day) is an essential component of haemoglobin that supplies oxygen to each cell of the human body. Iron deficiency leads to anaemia. Breast milk is not considered to be the best source of iron but it does supply iron in moderate quantity which is adequate for the infant till the age of 4 months.

5. **Folic acid** (150 mcg/day) is essential for the growth and development of the brain and spine of the baby. It also helps in the formation of new cells in the baby's body. Folic acid deficiency can also lead to anaemia in the mother.

6. **Vitamin C** (80 mg/day) is required for the formation of collagen and also for immunity against infections and diseases. Have vegetables in their raw form in delicious recipes like Cabbage and Moong Dal Salad (page 104) and Fruit and Lettuce Salad (page 100).

7. **Vitamin A** (Beta-carotene - 3800 mcg/day) is required for clear vision, skin and immunity. The requirement for vitamin A increases during lactation as the breast milk has appreciable amounts of this vitamin for the growing infant. Try Carrot Pancakes (page 145) which will satisfy your sweet tooth and fulfil your requirements of this vitamin.

8. **Vitamin D** is necessary as it aids the absorption of calcium in the body. As sunlight is a good source of vitamin D, dietary supplements are not required.

9. As compared to non-vegetarian foods, vegetarian diets are deficient in **Vitamin B12.** But don't let that worry you, as soya milk provides an appreciable amount of Vitamin B12.

10. Your diet should also include almonds, garlic, milk and garden cress (subza) seeds and methi (fenugreek) as these foods stimulate the production of breast milk. Baked Methi Puris (page 78), Garlic Roti (page 126) and Badam ka Sheera (page 151) are good choices.

A few words of caution from me about things you shouldn't do while breast feeding.

Don't forget that medication and food substances like caffeine pass through breast milk very easily and can affect your child's health. For that reason, check with your doctor/physician about the safety of the drugs you consume.

Avoid smoking and consumption of alcohol as they are detrimental for your baby's health.

Try to avoid carbonated drinks as these drinks provide empty kilocalories that are void of nutrients and only help to increase your weight.

Do continue your Calcium, Iron and Vitamin supplements, recommended by your obstetrician as they will benefit your baby through your breast milk.

Myths About Pregnancy

Don't do this.... and don't eat that......... I am sure you will hear these words more often while you're pregnant.

Your "saas" or shall I say mother-in-law believes that certain myths are true. But then again, they are also decades old. That's why I would like to help you differentiate between fact and fiction and most importantly between age-old myths and modern scientific breakthroughs. So let's erase these false notions and let the myths about pregnancy unfold...

MYTH	Eat for two
FACT	This is highly misleading. You don't really have to eat for two, but yes, you need to select healthy and nutritious foods during your pregnancy as your child is entirely dependent on you for its nourishment. Remember that quality is more important than quantity.
MYTH	The more weight you put on during your pregnancy, the healthier your baby will be
FACT	It is true that your weight gain is a good indicator of your baby's health but this doesn't mean that you should be overweight to have a healthy baby. The average weight gain should be between 10 to 12 kg. throughout your pregnancy. Your food cravings during pregnancy should not be an excuse to binge on all the wrong

foods that are unhealthy. You should select healthy foods to provide the best for your baby.

MYTH	Consumption of papaya leads to abortion
FACT	Papaya is considered to be a "hot" food and is believed to be harmful during pregnancy. But it's only raw papaya that is bad for you due to the presence of some enzymes which can cause uterine contractions during the first trimester. You can relish a well-ripened papaya during your later trimesters as it is a very good source of vitamin A and it serves as a laxative and diuretic.
MYTH	If you are anaemic, have plenty of beetroot
FACT	Many people believe beetroot is rich in iron as it is red in colour. This is a total misconception. The truly rich sources of iron are green leafy vegetables, dry fruits and oilseeds like til etc. Beetroot, however is rich in fibre, sugar and water so feel free to enjoy plenty of it.
MYTH	Citrus fruits aggravate acidity
FACT	Some women face acidity due to the consumption of citrus fruits. If you face this problem, do avoid eating them. However if you do not have acidity, continue to eat these fruits as they are recommended during pregnancy. Citrus fruits provide you with vitamin C and also have a high fibre content and will relieve you of constipation.
MYTH	A spoon of ghee daily eases your delivery
FACT	This is another false myth followed by most pregnant mothers. The excessive consumption of ghee will only make you fat without giving you any helping hand during delivery. Instead, you should continue your regular physical activities and exercises to tone your body as it will prove to be helpful during your time of labour. Walking and swimming are good form of exercises to be continued during pregnancy.

MYTH	Consuming dark coloured foods like tea and coffee makes your child dark
FACT	The complexion of your child is not at all dependent on the food you eat, but is entirely genetic. It's your partner's and your genes which help in the biological make-up of your baby. This myth was formed probably for those mothers who drink more than two cups of tea and coffee as these beverages are unhealthy due to their high caffeine content.
MYTH	Nursing mothers should have ghee, laddoos and other fatty foods to get plenty of breast milk
FACT	These foods will only make you put on weight. The quantity of milk is dependent on the amount of fluids you consume and by following a healthy diet of fruits, juices and soups. Your diet should include foods like almonds, fenugreek and garlic as these foods stimulate the production of breast milk.

Foods that Heal

They say "Old is Gold" (unlike the MYTHS) and that grandma's recipes are the best!!
Do you believe that? Well, I sure do.
This sentence does ring with truth.

Waltz right into the kitchen and try granny's home made remedies, designed especially to make you spring right back on your feet instead of being worn down by common illness.

Use the regular spices on your shelf rack as they are beneficial to your health and help tingle your taste buds too!!

Nature has the power
The power to cure and heal us
But many of us are oblivious to it
So keep your eyes wide open
and heal yourself with its bounty.

Coughs and colds

"aaacchooooooooo!!!!!!"
The onset of a cold has begun........

The following foods are used in our daily cooking and are great in getting rid of your cold and coughs.......

Turmeric (haldi): Turmeric is the best remedy for a cough. To ease a cough and cold, here are a few home remedies which will make you feel better.

Have a glass of hot milk after adding a pinch of turmeric powder and 1 tablespoon of honey. Have this 3 times a day and watch your cold vanish. For a sore throat and a cough, gargle with a glass of hot water to which a teaspoon of salt and ½ teaspoon of turmeric powder has been added.

Ginger: Ginger is an excellent remedy for coughs and colds, too.

In case of coughs, extracted juice of ginger with honey should be had three or four times a day. Add a teaspoon of freshly extracted ginger juice and a pinch of turmeric powder to a tablespoon of honey and feel your throat getting better.

To ease a cough, ginger should be cut into small pieces and boiled in a cup of water. It should then be strained, half a teaspoon of sugar added to it and the concoction should be drunk while it is hot.

Adding a few pieces of ginger into boiled water before adding tea leaves is what makes the famous Ginger Tea which helps to relieve colds.

Digestive disorders

Turmeric (haldi): Turmeric in small doses acts as an appetizer and will also help you out in case of indigestion. Use it in your daily cooking.

Fenugreek (methi): Fenugreek leaves are beneficial for overcoming indigestion and flatulence i.e. formation of gas. They also act as laxatives and are beneficial for relieving constipation related problems.

You can also have fenugreek seeds to relieve you from digestive disorders. Soak these seeds overnight and guzzle them down early the next morning with lukewarm water.

Ginger: Ginger is an indispensable drug for disorders of the digestive system. To ease vomiting and the formation of gas i.e. flatulence; chew on a piece of ginger after meals. You can also eat small pieces of ginger or sip its juice before meals to eliminate gas. Half a teaspoon of fresh ginger juice mixed with one teaspoon of fresh lime juice and mint juice constitutes an effective medicine for nausea and vomiting. If you like, add a tablespoon of honey!

Another delicious way to add ginger to your meals is to take fresh ginger, scrape the skin and cut it into thin slices. Put it in a sterelised bottle and add some salt and lemon juice to it. Mix well and refrigerate after 1 day. Have this delicious picked ginger with Bajra Khichdi (page 130).

Garlic: Garlic is one of the most beneficial foods which helps stimulate digestive juices that are essential for digestion. For all types of digestive disorders, crushed garlic cloves should be infused in water or milk and drink. Alternatively use it liberally in your daily cooking.

Anaemia

Iron is a basic constituent of haemoglobin that supplies oxygen to each cell of the human body. Insufficiency of iron will result in anaemia. If you are anaemic, eat fenugreek leaves and seeds as they are high in iron. You can also sip a tall glass of lime juice or squeeze lemon on your salad as the vitamin C content aids in the absorption of iron from your food. Have plenty of spinach, dates, sesame seeds etc.

....

Abbreviations Used:

The table below lists the abbreviations used in this book.

ABBREVIATIONS	
CHO	Carbohydrates
F.ACID	Folic acid
VIT.A	Vitamin A
VIT.C	Vitamin C
AMT	Amount
cm	Centimeters
gm	Grams
kcal	Kilocalories
kg	Kilograms
mcg	Micrograms
mg	Milligrams
ml	Millilitres

Recipes

Date and Banana Shake

This shake is a great way to start your day, especially during your first trimester when you may have lost your appetite as a result of morning sickness. The natural sweetness of the dates and bananas is enriched by the addition of milk and it provides for all the required calcium, protein and iron to supplement your diet.

If you are hungry or simply not in a mood to cook, you can be assured you will get all your nutrients, if you have just one serving of this revitalizer.

Prep. time : 15 min.   No cooking.   Serves 1.

¼ cup dates (khajur)
½ banana
1 cup milk
4 to 5 ice-cubes

1. Soak the dates in warm milk for 15 minutes.
2. Combine the soaked dates, milk and banana with 4 to 5 cubes of ice and blend in a liquidiser. Serve immediately.

Nutritive values per glass :

AMT	ENERGY	PROTEIN	CHO	FAT	VIT A	VIT C	CALCIUM	IRON	F.ACID	FIBRE
gm	kcal	gm	gm	gm	mcg	mg	mg	mg	mcg	gm
274	332	9.5	33.1	13.3	342.6	4.0	434.8	0.9	11.2	1.8

Pineapple Passion

This flavourful drink is one you should have after your first trimester has ended. Most doctors advice against having both papaya and pineapple fruits during the first trimester as these can sometimes cause complications. If you have water retention during your second trimester, both these fruits serve as a diuretic to flush your system.

Pineapple also adds to the content of iron, potassium, fibre and vitamin C.

Prep. time : 15 min.   No cooking.   Serves 1.

1 cup pineapple pieces, peeled and cubed
1 cup papaya pieces, peeled and cubed
1 tablespoon grated fresh coconut
2 to 3 ice-cubes

1. Blend the papaya pieces, pineapple pieces, coconut and ice-cubes in a liquidiser.
2. Pour into a tall glass.
   Serve immediately.

Handy tip   Ensure that both the papaya and pineapple are fully ripe so that they taste good and also do not upset your tummy.

Nutritive values per glass :

AMT	ENERGY	PROTEIN	CHO	FAT	VIT A	VIT C	CALCIUM	IRON	F.ACID	FIBRE
gm	kcal	gm	gm	gm	mcg	mg	mg	mg	mcg	gm
317	170	2.0	29.4	4.9	962.3	144.7	58.1	4.9	1.4	2.3

Guava Drink

Guava is a natural laxative as it is high in fibre and can help you if you're having digestive problems like constipation. This unusual concoction is a powerhouse of vitamin C and fibre. Have it with your afternoon snack to complement a chat-pata dish.

Remember to use fully ripened guavas as they taste the best and also you need to add less sugar to this drink thus making it more healthy.

Prep. time : 10 min.   Cooking time : 20 min.   Serves 6.

2 large guavas
¼ cup sugar
juice of ½ lemon
1 teaspoon ginger juice

1. Wash and cut the guavas into large cubes.
2. Place these in a saucepan along with the sugar and 1½ cups of water.
3. Bring to a boil and simmer till the guavas are tender.
4. Cool completely and purée in a blender.
5. Add the ginger juice and lemon juice and mix well.
6. Fill half a glass with the pulp and top up with chilled water or ice-cubes and serve immediately.
7. Repeat to make 5 more drinks.

Handy tips

1. You can also make a large batch when guavas are in season. Store the guava pulp in a sterilised bottle and refrigerate. Use as required.
2. The easiest way to make ginger juice is to grate the ginger and squeeze out the juice.

Nutritive values per glass :

AMT	ENERGY	PROTEIN	CHO	FAT	VIT A	VIT C	CALCIUM	IRON	F.ACID	FIBRE
gm	kcal	gm	gm	gm	mcg	mg	mg	mg	mcg	gm
31	40	0.2	9.5	0.1	0.0	46.9	3.9	0.1	0.0	1.2

Honey Banana Shake

Picture on page 57

This duo of bananas and yoghurt will provide for plenty of calcium and energy in your diet which is helpful throughout your 9 months of pregnancy. Be it early morning or mid afternoon, this refresher is sure to lift your spirits up.

Prep. time : 10 min.   No cooking.   Serves 1.

½ cup milk
½ cup fresh curds (yoghurt)
1 ripe banana, sliced
½ tablespoon honey

1. Combine the curds, banana, sugar, honey and ice-cubes in a blender until smooth.
2. Pour into 2 glasses and serve cold.

Nutritive values per glass :

AMT	ENERGY	PROTEIN	CHO	FAT	VIT A	VIT C	CALCIUM	IRON	F.ACID	FIBRE
gm	kcal	gm	gm	gm	mcg	mg	mg	mg	mcg	gm
267	331	9.6	33.7	13.2	364.5	6.1	434.7	0.7	11.5	0.3

Fig and Apricot Shake

Picture on page 57

This shake is best had early in the morning for breakfast as your body conserves more nutrients at this time of the day. Packed with iron, fibre, protein and natural sugar, these dry fruits will provide you with energy and will also satiate your hunger.

Prep. time : 30 min.   No cooking.   Serves 1.

5 slices of dried figs
4 dried apricots, deseeded
1 cup milk
4 to 5 ice-cubes

1. Soak the figs and apricots in warm milk for at least ½ hour.
2. Combine the milk and dried fruits in a liquidiser along with the ice-cubes and blend.
   Serve immediately.

Nutritive values per glass :

AMT	ENERGY	PROTEIN	CHO	FAT	VIT A	VIT C	CALCIUM	IRON	F.ACID	FIBRE
gm	kcal	gm	gm	gm	mcg	mg	mg	mg	mcg	gm
247	284	9.2	21.5	13.2	383.7	4.0	461.2	1.3	11.2	1.1

My Fair Lady

Picture on page 75

This magic formula is rich in energy and protein. The addition of yoghurt makes this a delightful drink and a good source of calcium and protein too. You can try this soothing drink for a warm afternoon to soothe the heat away.

Prep. time : 5 min.   No cooking.   Serves 1.

½ cup black grapes
½ cup fresh curds (yoghurt)
½ cup milk
crushed ice to serve

1. Blend all the ingredients together in a liquidiser, adding some water if the mixture is too thick.
2. Serve chilled with crushed ice.

Nutritive values per glass :

AMT	ENERGY	PROTEIN	CHO	FAT	VIT A	VIT C	CALCIUM	IRON	F.ACID	FIBRE
gm	kcal	gm	gm	gm	mcg	mg	mg	mg	mcg	gm
270	284	9.0	21.6	13.2	320.0	2.7	434.0	0.8	11.2	2.0

Strawberry Chickoo Shake

Picture on page 57

This is one of my favourite breakfast shakes. When I am in a hurry, I simply gulp it down and rush out. Packed with protein, calcium, iron, vitamin C and fibre too, this is a delicious drink.

Prep. time : 5 min.   No cooking.   Serves 2.

½ cup ripe strawberries, chopped
½ cup chickoo, peeled and diced
1 cup milk

1. Combine all the ingredients and blend in a liquidiser.
2. Pour into 2 glasses.
   Serve chilled.

Handy tip

For best results, ensure that all the ingredients are chilled.

Nutritive values per glass :

AMT	ENERGY	PROTEIN	CHO	FAT	VIT A	VIT C	CALCIUM	IRON	F.ACID	FIBRE
gm	kcal	gm	gm	gm	mcg	mg	mg	mg	mcg	gm
204	198	5.0	22.8	7.3	230.9	24.7	239.9	1.7	5.6	2.1

Breakfast

Dal and Vegetable Idli

These nutritious idlis are slightly heavier than the regular idlis as the batter is not fermented.

They are very nutritive because of the combination of 3 dals and vegetables like methi, green peas and carrots. These are great for an early pregnancy boost and being an excellent source of iron, fibre, folic acid and vitamin C, they will ensure that you and your baby get plenty of goodness.

You can even make sumptuous pancakes with the same batter instead of steaming them into idlis.

Prep. time : 15 min. Cooking time : 10 to 12 min.
Makes 6 idlis.

½ cup toovar (arhar) dal
¼ cup split yellow gram (yellow moong dal)
½ cup split Bengal gram (chana dal)
1 cup fenugreek (methi) leaves, chopped
2 cups chopped coriander
¼ cup green peas, boiled and mashed
¼ cup grated coconut
3 green chillies, chopped
1 small onion, chopped
1 small carrot, grated
salt to taste
1 teaspoon oil for greasing

1. Wash and soak the dals together at least 3 hours.
2. Drain and grind to a smooth paste, adding a little water. Add the fenugreek, coriander, green peas, coconut, green chillies, onion, carrot and salt.
3. Add water as required to make a thick batter.
4. Pour into greased idli moulds and steam for 10 to 12 minutes till done.
5. Serve hot with coconut chutney.

Nutritive values per idli :

AMT	ENERGY	PROTEIN	CHO	FAT	VIT A	VIT C	CALCIUM	IRON	F.ACID	FIBRE
gm	kcal	gm	gm	gm	mcg	mg	mg	mg	mcg	gm
78	166	8.8	24.4	3.8	875.4	16.0	69.8	1.9	46.0	1.1

Soya Upma

Whip up this nutritive upma that is loaded with vegetables and is also much more nutritious than plain semolina upma.

Soya bean granules are smaller version of nuggets. If you are using nuggets instead of granules, chop them into really small pieces after boiling them.

Vegetarian diets are deficient in Vitamin B12, but soyabean and its by-products are an excellent vegetarian source of this vitamin. Soya granules and nuggets provide plenty of protein, energy and calcium too. Lemon juice provides good vitamin C and also aids the absorption of iron from food.

Prep. time : 20 min.   Cooking time : 10 min.   Serves 4.

$^3/_4$ cup soya granules
1 teaspoon cumin seeds (jeera)
1 tablespoon urad dal (split black lentils)
$^1/_4$ teaspoon asafoetida (hing)
1 teaspoon grated ginger
1 to 2 green chillies, slit
1 onion, chopped
$^1/_2$ cup grated carrot
$^1/_2$ cup cabbage, chopped
juice of $^1/_2$ lemon
1 tablespoon oil
salt to taste

For the garnish
2 tablespoons chopped coriander

1. Soak the soya granules in hot water for approximately 15 minutes. Drain, squeeze out all the water and keep aside.
2. Heat the oil in a pan and add the cumin seeds. When they crackle, add the urad dal and sauté till the dal turns light brown.
3. Add the asafoetida, ginger, green chillies and onion.
4. Sauté the onion pieces till they are translucent. Then add the carrot and cabbage and sauté for 4 to 5 minutes.
5. Add the soya granules and mix well.
6. Season with salt and lemon juice.
7. Mix well and serve hot garnished with chopped coriander.

Nutritive values per serving :

AMT	ENERGY	PROTEIN	CHO	FAT	VIT A	VIT C	CALCIUM	IRON	F.ACID	FIBRE
gm	kcal	gm	gm	gm	mcg	mg	mg	mg	mcg	gm
63	107	5.5	8.2	5.8	400.4	18.7	55.5	1.5	18.9	0.8

Moong Dal Dosa

The cereal and pulse combination makes this recipe a good source of quality protein. These thin, crisp dosas made of moong dal and rice make a terrific breakfast especially during your first trimester. The fibre and vitamin content of the recipe is also good due to the addition of parboiled rice.
Parboiled rice is a thick variety of unpolished rice that is used to make South Indian snacks like idlis and dosas.

Prep. time : 10 min.   Soaking time : 3 hours.
Fermenting time : 8 hours.   Cooking time : 25 min.
Makes 11 dosas.

1 cup split green gram (green moong dal)
1 cup parboiled rice (ukda rice)
salt to taste
6 teaspoons oil for cooking (approx. ½ teaspoon per dosa)

1. Wash and soak the moong dal and rice in water for at least 3 hours. Drain.
2. Grind to a fine paste using a little water.
3. Cover and allow to ferment for at least 8 hours.
4. Add the salt and adjust the consistency of the batter by adding water if required. Mix well.
5. The batter should be of a dropping consistency.
6. Heat and grease a non-stick tava with oil.
7. Pour a ladleful of the batter on the tava and spread it using a circular motion, to make a thin pancake.
8. Drizzle a little oil on the sides and cook.
9. When the lower side is golden brown, fold over.
10. Repeat with the remaining batter to make more dosas.
   Serve hot with chutney.

Handy tip Parboiled rice is a variety of rice used especially to make idlis and dosas. It is available at most grocery shops.

Nutritive values per dosa :

AMT	ENERGY	PROTEIN	CHO	FAT	VIT A	VIT C	CALCIUM	IRON	F.ACID	FIBRE
gm	kcal	gm	gm	gm	mcg	mg	mg	mg	mcg	gm
35	150	4.4	21.2	5.2	51.8	0.0	11.8	0.7	21.1	0.1

Methi Palak Dhoklas

These quick and easy to make dhoklas are best enjoyed as a breakfast dish or even a late afternoon snack. Black-eyed beans, also called cow peas, or chawli beans are extremely rich in iron and folic acid. Both these nutrients are required in abundance, especially during the first trimester.

Prep. time : 10 min.   Cooking time : 20 min.
Soaking time : 6 hours.   Serves 4.

1 cup black-eyed beans (chawli)
¾ cup chopped spinach (palak)
¾ cup chopped fenugreek (methi) leaves
2 tablespoons oil
1 tablespoon green chilli-ginger paste
1½ teaspoons asafoetida (hing)
1 tablespoon Eno's fruit salt
salt to taste

1. Wash and soak the beans for at least 6 hours. Drain.
2. Add approximately ¾ cup of water and blend in a liquidiser to make a smooth batter.
3. Add the spinach, fenugreek, oil, green chilli-ginger paste, asafoetida and salt and mix well into a batter.
4. Put the steamer on the gas and when the water in the steamer starts to boil, add the fruit salt into the batter and mix well.
5. Pour the batter into 3 greased thalis, put them in the steamer and steam for 8 to 10 minutes.
6. Serve hot with green chutney.

1. **Honey Banana Shake,** *page 49*
2. **Fig and Apricot Shake,** *page 49*
3. **Strawberry Chickoo Shake,** *page 51*
4. **Chocolate Chip and Oatmeal Cookies,** *page 69*

Handy tips

1. Add the fruit salt into the batter just before you are ready to steam the dhoklas, or the dhoklas will not rise.
2. Remember that the water in the steamer should be boiling when you put in the dhoklas to steam.

Nutritive values per serving :

AMT	ENERGY	PROTEIN	CHO	FAT	VIT A	VIT C	CALCIUM	IRON	F.ACID	FIBRE
gm	kcal	gm	gm	gm	mcg	mg	mg	mg	mcg	gm
66	203	10.1	22.3	8.0	906.4	6.3	60.8	3.7	68.9	1.7

Bulgur Wheat Pancakes

Bulgur wheat proves to be a good breakfast food as it provides an adequate amount of energy (calories) and protein. Since your body requires calcium, the addition of curds improves the calcium content of the recipe. These pancakes are ideal for your second trimester as they are rich in fibre and will ease your digestive problems too.

Prep. time : 20 min.   Cooking time : 15 min.
                                      Makes 10 pancakes.

1½ cups fine bulgur wheat (dalia)
2 tablespoons whole wheat flour (gehun ka atta)
½ cup fresh curds (yoghurt)
1 cup finely chopped cabbage
2 green chillies, chopped

1. Banana Walnut Pancakes, *page 62*

2 teaspoons oil
¼ teaspoon asafoetida (hing)
salt to taste
approx. 3 tablespoons oil for cooking

1. Soak the bulgur wheat in hot water for 10 to 15 minutes. Drain completely.
2. In a large bowl, combine all the ingredients and mix well. Add a little water (approx. ¼ cup) to make a thick batter.
3. Prepare small pancakes on a non-stick frying pan using a little oil to cook both sides, till they are golden brown.
   Serve hot with green chutney.

Nutritive values per pancake :

AMT	ENERGY	PROTEIN	CHO	FAT	VIT A	VIT C	CALCIUM	IRON	F.ACID	FIBRE
gm	kcal	gm	gm	gm	mcg	mg	mg	mg	mcg	gm
48	153	2.6	19.3	7.0	80.4	10.3	33.3	1.3	3.1	0.5

Buckwheat Pancake

Buckwheat is called "Kutti-no daro" in Gujarati and "kutto" in most other Indian languages. This recipe is a variation of a traditional recipe and is modified to make it healthier by using much oil and adding potatoes to add softness to the texture of this dish.

It is made into a big pancake and then cut into wedges before serving with fresh coriander chutney.

Buckwheat is high in iron and fibre while the curds contribute calcium and protein and potatoes provide carbohydrates and energy in this recipe.

This recipe is recommended for the third trimester because your energy requirements are higher during this period.

Prep. time : 2 hours.   Cooking time : 15 minutes.
                                       Makes 6 wedges.

1 cup buckwheat (kutto, kutti no daro)
1 cup grated raw potato
1 cup curds (yoghurt)
1 tablespoon grated ginger
2 to 3 green chillies, chopped
¼ cup chopped coriander
salt to taste

For the tempering
3 tablespoons oil
1 teaspoon cumin seeds (jeera)
1½ teaspoons sesame seeds (til)
¼ teaspoon asafoetida (hing)

1. Combine the buckwheat and curds in a large bowl and mix well. Allow to stand for 1 hour.
2. Then add the grated potato, ginger, green chillies, coriander and salt and mix well. Allow to stand for 1 more hour.
3. Heat the oil in a non-stick pan which is approximately 150 mm. (6") in diameter.
4. Add the cumin seeds and when they crackle, add the sesame seeds and the asafoetida.
5. Pour the buckwheat batter in an even layer and cover the pan.
6. Lower the gas flame and allow it to cook for 5 to 7 minutes till the bottom is golden brown in colour.
7. Lift the pancake gently using 2 large flat spoons and turn it over to the other side.
8. Cook again for 4 to 5 minutes.
9. Cut into six wedges and serve hot.

Nutritive values per wedge :

AMT	ENERGY	PROTEIN	CHO	FAT	VIT A	VIT C	CALCIUM	IRON	F.ACID	FIBRE
gm	kcal	gm	gm	gm	mcg	mg	mg	mg	mcg	gm
77	156	4.2	20.7	5.5	149.2	4.4	95.6	3.8	3.0	2.1

Banana Walnut Pancakes

Picture on page 58

These delicious breakfast pancakes are enriched with wheat bran, bananas and milk and are perfect for brunch. Bananas and milk provide you with all the energy needed to carry out your regular activities. They also increase the calcium and protein levels of the recipe. Most of us consider waffles and pancakes to be really sinful indulgences. It is actually the ingredients we eat with them like butter, jam or honey that actually make them full of calories. Go ahead and dab a little butter on your pancakes but remember it is an indulgence that should not be overdone.

Prep. time : 10 min.   Cooking time : 10 min.
Makes 4 pancakes.

1 cup whole wheat flour (gehun ka atta)
2 tablespoons wheat bran
2 ripe bananas
½ cup walnuts, finely chopped
½ cup milk
4 tablespoons castor sugar
½ teaspoon vanilla essence
½ teaspoon baking powder
1 tablespoon melted butter

Other ingredients
4 teaspoons butter to cook
honey or jam to serve
sliced banana to serve

1. Mash 1 banana and slice the other one.
2. Combine all the ingredients except the sliced banana in a bowl with approximately ½ cup of water. Mix well to make a smooth batter making sure that no lumps remain. Keep aside.

3. Heat a non-stick pan, spread about 3 to 4 tablespoons (¼ cup) of the batter to make a thick pancake of about 100 mm. (4") diameter. Place a few slices of bananas on top.
4. Cook the pancake over medium heat using a little butter to cook on both sides until golden brown.
5. Repeat the same for the remaining batter to make 3 more pancakes.
   Serve hot with honey or jam.

Nutritive values per pancake :

AMT	ENERGY	PROTEIN	CHO	FAT	VIT A	VIT C	CALCIUM	IRON	F.ACID	FIBRE
gm	kcal	gm	gm	gm	mcg	mg	mg	mg	mcg	gm
117	363	7.6	43.0	17.2	247.0	2.2	89.5	2.3	17.5	1.3

Snacks

Golpapdi

These serve as a good snack in the evening and can even be the best thing to have early in the morning when you feel a little nauseous. Jaggery, apart from being a good source of iron, acts as an instant "pick me up".

Although ghee is a good source of vitamin A, it should be had in moderation because it contains a lot of saturated fat which is not good for you.

Prep. time : 10 min.   Cooking time : 20 min.
                                            Makes 24 pieces.

1 cup whole wheat flour (gehun ka atta)
¾ cup jaggery (gur), cut into small pieces
1 teaspoon poppy seeds (khus khus)
¼ teaspoon cardamom (elaichi) powder
1 teaspoon desiccated coconut
5 tablespoons ghee

1. Sprinkle the poppy seeds on a 150 mm. (6") diameter greased thali. Keep aside.
2. Melt the ghee in a frying pan and add the wheat flour, stirring continuously till it turns golden brown in colour.
3. Remove from the flame, cool slightly and add the jaggery, cardamom powder and coconut. Stir well.
4. When the jaggery melts and the mixture is still warm, pour it into the greased thali with poppy seeds and spread it evenly with the help of the base of a small bowl (katori).
5. Cut into 24 pieces while still warm.
6. Store in an air-tight container when cool.

Handy tip

You can add 1 tablespoon of milk along with the jaggery if the mixture becomes too hard.

Variation :

Gaund Golpapdi
(for lactation)

Gaund is a very traditional ingredient that is given to lactating mothers as it is supposed to aid in the production of breast milk and also strengthens your back after delivery. It also adds some crunch to an old classic recipe!

Roast ¼ cup of gaund (edible gum) over a medium flame till it puffs up. Allow it to cool completely. Add 1 teaspoon of soonth (dry ginger powder) and crumble this mixture using a mortar and pestle till it is almost powdered.
Add this mixture to the above recipe at step 3 and proceed as above.

Nutritive values per piece :

AMT	ENERGY	PROTEIN	CHO	FAT	VIT A	VIT C	CALCIUM	IRON	F.ACID	FIBRE
gm	kcal	gm	gm	gm	mcg	mg	mg	mg	mcg	gm
12	59	0.6	7.7	2.9	25.7	0.0	8.5	0.4	1.6	0.1

Whole Wheat Methi Khakhras

These make an excellent substitute for biscuits. Whole wheat provides excellent fibre to relieve your digestive problems. Methi increases the iron and calcium content of the recipe.
Have these for your early morning dry carbohydrate snack during the first trimester, as they will help keep nausea at bay. Have them early in the morning before your breakfast.

Prep. time : 10 min.   Cooking time : 20 min.
                           Makes 15 khakhras.

1½ cups whole wheat flour (gehun ka atta)
¾ cup finely chopped fenugreek (methi) leaves
1 teaspoon ajwain (carom seeds)
1 teaspoon sesame seeds (til)
¼ teaspoon chilli powder
¼ teaspoon turmeric powder (haldi)

2 teaspoons oil
salt to taste

1. To the fenugreek leaves, add the ajwain, sesame seeds, chilli powder, turmeric powder, oil and salt and mix well for 2 minutes until the leaves become soft.
2. Add the flour and knead into a dough, adding just enough water to make a firm dough.
3. Divide the dough into 15 portions and roll out each portion into very thin circles, using a little flour.
4. Cook one portion lightly for a few seconds on both sides on a tava (griddle).
5. Apply a little ghee or oil on the khakhra.
6. Repeat for the remaining portions.
7. Cook again on a slow flame until crisp using a little pressure with help of a cloth.
8. Cool and store in an air-tight jar.

Nutritive values per khakhra :

AMT	ENERGY	PROTEIN	CHO	FAT	VIT A	VIT C	CALCIUM	IRON	F.ACID	FIBRE
gm	kcal	gm	gm	gm	mcg	mg	mg	mg	mcg	gm
13	44	1.4	7.6	0.9	42.0	0.7	12.6	0.6	3.9	0.2

Til Chikki

Making chikki is a tricky process and you may find yourself wasting a batch or two till you get the hang of it. Once you are able to make chikki easily, then you can make larger quantities at one time and store them in an air-tight container.

You can also use other ingredients like peanuts, almonds, and cashew for more variations of chikki. I chose "til" (sesame seeds) as it is the most nutritious.

Til chikki is very nutritious because of the combination of sesame seeds and jaggery, both of which are good sources of iron. Whenever you feel nauseous, have just one piece and you will feel better. Til is a good source of protein and iron.

Prep. time : 10 min.   Cooking time : 10 min.
                              Makes 10 pieces.

½ cup sesame seeds (til)
⅓ cup jaggery (gur)
1 teaspoon ghee

Other ingredients
½ teaspoon ghee for greasing

1. Roast the sesame seeds till they are light golden in colour. Cool and keep aside.
2. In the meantime, grease the back of flat thali with a little ghee and keep it aside.
3. Heat the ghee in a pan and add the jaggery to it.
4. Simmer over a slow flame till it caramelises and forms a hard ball when you add a drop in cold water.
5. Add the roasted til and mix it thoroughly with the melted jaggery. You may need to put out the flame during this process.
6. When the mixture is ready, pour the entire mixture over the greased thali or a smooth stone surface. Roll it out into thin sheets using a greased rolling pin.
7. When cool, cut into square pieces. Store in an air-tight container.

Handy tip

A special variety of jaggery is available at some grocery stores that is used in the making of chikki.
It is dark brown in colour and is soft in texture. If that is not available, you can use regular jaggery.

Nutritive values per piece :

AMT	ENERGY	PROTEIN	CHO	FAT	VIT A	VIT C	CALCIUM	IRON	F.ACID	FIBRE
gm	kcal	gm	gm	gm	mcg	mg	mg	mg	mcg	gm
12	57	1.1	6.3	3.1	8.1	0.0	91.0	0.7	0.0	0.2

Bajra Khakhras

During your first trimester, it is better to have dry carbohydrates for your breakfast to ease morning sickness. If you are fed up of regular biscuits and breads, try these crunchy khakhras instead. Make these in large batches so that you can have them in the mornings whenever you have the urge to eat something. The addition of til improves the iron content of these khakhras.

Prep. time : 10 min.   Cooking time : 25 min.
                              Makes 7 khakhras.

½ cup bajra flour (black millet flour)
2 tablespoons whole wheat flour (gehun ka atta)
½ teaspoon ginger-garlic paste
¼ teaspoon green chillies, finely chopped
½ teaspoon sesame seeds (til)
¼ teaspoon turmeric powder (haldi)
1 teaspoon oil
ghee for cooking
salt to taste

1. Combine the bajra flour, whole wheat flour, ginger-garlic paste, green chillies, sesame seeds, turmeric powder, oil and salt .
2. Add enough warm water and knead well into a firm dough.
3. Divide the dough into 7 equal portions and roll each on a floured surface into a 75 mm. (3") diameter thin circle.
4. Cook on a hot tava (griddle) on both the sides with a little ghee until pink spots appear on top of the rolled out dough.
5. With the help of a folded muslin cloth, press the khakhra from all sides and cook till crisp, over a slow flame.
6. Repeat for the remaining to make 6 more khakhras.
7. Cool and store in an air-tight container.

You can also add 1 to 2 tablespoon of finely chopped methi leaves (fenugreek) into the dough to make Bajra Methi Khakhras.

Nutritive values per khakhra :

AMT	ENERGY	PROTEIN	CHO	FAT	VIT A	VIT C	CALCIUM	IRON	F.ACID	FIBRE
gm	kcal	gm	gm	gm	mcg	mg	mg	mg	mcg	gm
13	66	1.1	6.4	4.0	42.0	0.0	6.2	0.7	4.0	0.1

Chocolate Chip and Oatmeal Cookies

Picture on page 57

Chocolate chip cookies are usually considered to be a sinful indulgence. This recipe is not one of those as it so adds iron, protein and fibre to your diet, while pampering your palate with delicious chocolate chips. Have these with a glass of warm milk and you will surely feel better.

Prep. time : 10 min. Baking time : 25 to 30 min.
Makes 12 cookies. Baking temperature : 160°C (320°F).

1 cup quick cooking rolled oats
⅔ cup whole wheat flour (gehun ka atta)
¾ cup butter, softened
½ cup grated apple
4 tablespoons brown sugar
1 teaspoon vanilla essence
¼ cup chocolate chips or chopped chocolate

1. Combine all the ingredients except the chocolate chips in a bowl and knead into a dough.
2. When it is ready, add the chocolate chips and knead the dough lightly again.
3. Refrigerate the dough for 15 to 20 minutes and divide it into 12 equal portions.
4. Roll out each portion into a round and flatten it

between your palms to make a circle of approximately 6 mm. (¼") thickness.

5. Place on a baking tray and bake in a pre-heated oven at 160°C (320°F) for 25 to 30 minutes or till the cookies are golden brown.

6. Cool completely and store in an air-tight container.

Nutritive values per cookie :

AMT	ENERGY	PROTEIN	CHO	FAT	VIT A	VIT C	CALCIUM	IRON	F.ACID	FIBRE
gm	kcal	gm	gm	gm	mcg	mg	mg	mg	mcg	gm
33	151	1.8	12.8	10.8	338.1	0.0	8. 6	0.7	4.3	0.4

Sprout and Fruit Bhel

Picture on page 75

Want to eat chat-pata? Try this new version of bhel. Your energy and protein requirements shoot up during the second trimester and also you may sometimes feel like munching on a snack. This is an excellent snack with a good combination of sprouts and fruits providing you with vitamins and fibre.

Prep. time : 10 min.   Cooking time : 10 min.   Serves 4.

For the sev-mamara
1 cup mamara (puffed rice)
½ cup sev
½ teaspoon cumin seeds (jeera)
a pinch asafoetida (hing)
¼ teaspoon turmeric powder (haldi)
¼ teaspoon black salt (sanchal)
½ teaspoon oil

Other ingredients
4 tablespoons peanuts, boiled
4 tablespoons moong sprouts
4 tablespoons chopped tomato
4 tablespoons chopped apple
2 tablespoons chopped raw mango

4 tablespoons fresh pomegranate seeds
½ cup orange segments
4 tablespoons chopped coriander
4 teaspoons lemon juice
salt to taste

For the sev-mamara
1. Heat the oil and add the cumin seeds. When they crackle, add the asafoetida, turmeric powder and mamara and mix well.
2. Add the black salt and sev, mix well and cool completely.
3. Store in an air-tight container and use as required.

How to proceed
Mix all the ingredients together and serve immediately.

Nutritive values per serving :

AMT	ENERGY	PROTEIN	CHO	FAT	VIT A	VIT C	CALCIUM	IRON	F.ACID	FIBRE
gm	kcal	gm	gm	gm	mcg	mg	mg	mg	mcg	gm
110	231	9.8	28.6	8.6	714.3	20.4	62. 6	2.3	22.9	2.1

High Fibre Bread

Picture on page 102

This is a good alternative to white bread that is made using refined flour. It is not as soft as white bread, but it does have a rich earthy taste and is crumbly. I love toasting the slices and smearing strawberry jam over them.

During the second trimester, your appetite will increase and you may also start having digestive problems. This bread is full of fibre and protein which will satisfy your appetite and can also help to relieve your constipation problems.

Wheat bran is available at large supermarkets or at health food stores.

Prep. time : 15 min.   Baking time : 45 min.
Baking temperature : 160°C (320°F).
Makes 1 loaf (approx.12 slices)

1²/₃ cups whole wheat flour (gehun ka atta)
1³/₄ cups quick cooking rolled oats
2¹/₄ cups wheat bran
³/₄ cup softened butter
salt to taste
1 teaspoon oil for greasing

1. Combine the flour, oats and wheat bran in a large bowl and mix well.
2. Add the butter and salt and rub it into the flour using your fingertips till the butter is evenly distributed in the flour mixture.
3. Add 1½ cups of water and knead into a dough.
4. Add the oil and knead again.
5. Roll the dough into a long loaf approximately 75 mm. (3") in width and place on a greased baking tray.
6. Bake in a pre-heated oven at 160°C (320°C) for 45 minutes till the crust is golden brown in colour.
7. Cool and cut into slices.

Variation :

High Fibre Bhakhri

I also made bhakhris out of this dough and I enjoyed them with vegetable. Make them exactly as you would make parathas over a slow flame but do not add oil to cook them as the dough has plenty of butter. You can make about 20 bhakhris by dividing the dough into equal portions.

Nutritive values per slice :

AMT	ENERGY	PROTEIN	CHO	FAT	VIT A	VIT C	CALCIUM	IRON	F.ACID	FIBRE
gm	kcal	gm	gm	gm	mcg	mg	mg	mg	mcg	gm
46	206	4.9	23.2	10.5	343.9	0.0	24.5	2.6	35.3	1.6

Thalipeeth

A nutritious pancake made with 3 kinds of flours, making it delicious and more importantly nutritious also. Thalipeeth is the easiest snack that you can make. The iron and folic acid content of the recipe is high and will help supplement your needs during the first trimester. You can also use a combination of any of other flours like bajra, besan and rice flour if you wish.

Prep. time : 4 min.   Cooking time : 7 min.
                        Makes 4 thalipeeth.

3 tablespoons Bengal gram flour (besan)
3 tablespoons jowar flour (white millet flour)
3 tablespoons whole wheat flour (gehun ka atta)
1 small onion, chopped
1 tomato, chopped
2 tablespoons chopped coriander
2 green chillies, finely chopped
salt to taste

Other ingredients
1 tablespoon sesame seeds (til)
2 teaspoons oil for cooking

1. Mix together all the ingredients in a bowl and add enough water to make a thick batter.
2. Heat and grease a non-stick tava (griddle).
3. Spread a layer of the batter to form a pancake of 4 mm. (1/") thickness and sprinkle some sesame seeds on top.
4. Cook on both sides till golden brown, using a little oil.
5. Repeat to make 3 more thalipeeth.
   Serve hot with green chutney.

Handy tip

You can add almost any flour that is on your kitchen shelf like bajra flour, rice flour, nachni flour etc. to make thalipeeth.

Nutritive values per thalipeeth :

AMT	ENERGY	PROTEIN	CHO	FAT	VIT A	VIT C	CALCIUM	IRON	F.ACID	FIBRE
gm	kcal	gm	gm	gm	mcg	mg	mg	mg	mcg	gm
67	140	3.6	16.2	6.7	231.2	9.5	65.7	1.4	19.5	0.7

Mooli Muthias

Steamed radish dumplings make a delicious and nutritious snack.

Radish is one vegetable that most of us ignore inspite of it being a very good source of calcium, vitamins A and C and fibre. This recipe is a delicious way to include this much-ignored vegetable in your diet. If you don't want to make these dumplings with radish, use grated bottle gourd (doodhi/lauki) instead.

Prep. time : 10 min.   Cooking time : 15 min.   Serves 2.

1 cup grated radish with the stems and leaves (finely chopped)
½ cup Bengal gram flour (besan)
½ cup jowar flour (white millet flour)
2 tablespoons curds (yoghurt)
1 tablespoon chopped coriander
juice of ½ lemon
1 teaspoon oil
1 teaspoon green chilli-ginger paste

1. My Fair Lady, *page 50*
2. Sprout and Fruit Bhel, *page 70*

2 large cloves garlic, grated
½ teaspoon turmeric powder (haldi)
1 tablespoon sugar (optional)
salt to taste

For the tempering
1 teaspoon cumin seeds (jeera)
1 teaspoon sesame seeds (til)
¼ teaspoon asafoetida (hing)
1½ tablespoons oil

For the garnish
2 tablespoons chopped coriander

Other ingredients
oil for greasing

1. Combine all the ingredients in a bowl and knead to make batter-like soft dough.
2. Divide into 3 equal parts and roll each portion into a cylindrical shape approximately 125 mm. (5") in length.
3. Place on a greased steaming dish and steam for 10 to 12 minutes till firm.
4. Remove, cool and cut into 25 mm. (1") thick slices.

1. Lentil and Vegetable Broth, *page 81*
2. Stir Fry Salad, *page 97*

How to proceed

1. Heat the oil in a pan and add the cumin seeds. When they crackle, add the asafoetida and sesame seeds.
2. Add the sliced muthias and sauté over a low flame till they are lightly browned.
3. Serve hot, garnished with the coriander leaves.

Nutritive values per serving :

AMT	ENERGY	PROTEIN	CHO	FAT	VIT A	VIT C	CALCIUM	IRON	F.ACID	FIBRE
gm	kcal	gm	gm	gm	mcg	mg	mg	mg	mcg	gm
125	342	8.4	33.2	19.2	946.5	19.1	112.9	2.4	36.0	1.1

Baked Methi Puris

Methi helps in the production of breast milk and should therefore be consumed during your time of lactation. Minimal usage of oil makes this recipe enjoyable to eat without the guilt of indulging in the original fried version of puris. These baked puris moreover provide for iron and calcium in your diet.

These also make a great snack in your first trimester as it is another carbohydrate rich recipe.

Prep. time : 15 min.   Baking time : 1 hour.
Makes 30 puris.   Baking temperature : 180°C (360°F).

1 cup whole wheat flour (gehun ka atta)
½ cup chopped fenugreek (methi) leaves
½ teaspoon turmeric powder (haldi)
1 teaspoon chilli powder
1 teaspoon coriander-cumin seeds (dhania-jeera) powder
1 teaspoon oil
salt to taste
oil for greasing

1. Combine all the ingredients and knead into a firm dough using as much water as required.
2. Divide the dough into 30 equal portions and roll out each portion into a circle of about 75 mm. (3") diameter.
3. Place on a greased baking tray and prick all over using a fork.
4. Bake in a pre-heated oven at 180°C (360°F) for 10 to 15 minutes or till the puris are golden brown, turning them around once.
5. Cool and store in an air-tight container.

Handy tip To make the puris crisp, the dough should be really firm.

Nutritive values per puri :

AMT	ENERGY	PROTEIN	CHO	FAT	VIT A	VIT C	CALCIUM	IRON	F.ACID	FIBRE
gm	kcal	gm	gm	gm	mcg	mcg	mg	mg	mcg	gm
5	17	0.5	2.5	0.6	16.5	0.2	3.6	0.2	1.3	0.1

Mukhwaas (kankari ajwain)

Almonds and gaund are foods that help to increase the production of milk.

This mixture is traditionally made for lactating mothers and is supposed to be had once or twice a day to help relieve you from digestive problems like gas or flatulence. All the ingredients have therapeutic properties and so even if you don't much care for its taste, have it like medicine or as a mouth freshener.

Prep. time : 5 min.   Cooking time : 10 min.   Makes 1 cup.

1 tablespoon gaund (edible gum)
1 tablespoon ajwain (carom seeds)
1 tablespoon fennel seeds (saunf)
1 teaspoon sesame seeds (til)
1 teaspoon poppy seeds (khus-khus)

1 tablespoon almonds, sliced
2 tablespoons dry coconut (kopra)
2 tablespoons powdered sugar
1 tablespoon ghee

1. Heat the ghee, add the gaund pieces and sauté till they puff up.
2. Add the ajwain, fennel, sesame seeds, poppy seeds, almonds and dry coconut and sauté over a slow flame till all the ingredients release their aroma.
3. Allow to cool completely and break down the gaund to smaller pieces.
4. Add the sugar and mix well.
5. Store in an air-tight container.

Handy tip You can have 2 teaspoons of this mixture after lunch and dinner while you are lactating.

Nutritive values for 2 teaspoons :

AMT	ENERGY	PROTEIN	CHO	FAT	VIT A	VIT C	CALCIUM	IRON	F.ACID	FIBRE
gm	kcal	gm	gm	gm	mcg	mg	mg	mg	mcg	gm
8	45	0.7	3.3	3.3	11.4	0.1	30.2	0.4	0.2	0.1

Soups

Lentil and Vegetable Broth

Picture on page 76

This broth is a nutritious combination of dal and vegetables which is good for your first trimester. Tomatoes and spinach provide iron and folic acid which are essential during this trimester and cheese and lentils are a good source of protein.

Being a mildly flavoured soup, it will stimulate your appetite if you're nauseous and will also nourish you.

Prep. time : 20 min.   Cooking time : 20 min.   Serves 4.

For the stock
2 tablespoons yellow moong dal (split yellow gram), washed
2 onions
2 large tomatoes

For the topping
1 chopped onion
1/3 cup shredded cabbage
1/3 cup chopped spinach (palak)
4 tablespoons tomato ketchup
1 tomato, chopped
1 tablespoon oil
salt and pepper to taste

To serve
grated cheese and spring onion greens

For the stock
1. Cut the onions and tomatoes into big pieces.
2. Add the moong dal and 4 cups of water and cook in a pressure cooker.
3. When cooked, cool completely. Blend in a liquidiser and keep aside.

How to proceed

1. Heat the oil and sauté the onion for 1 minute.
2. Add the cabbage and spinach and sauté again for 1 minute.
3. Add the stock and simmer for 10 minutes.
4. Add the ketchup, chopped tomato, salt and pepper and bring to a boil.

   Serve hot with grated cheese and spring onion greens.

Nutritive values per serving :

AMT	ENERGY	PROTEIN	CHO	FAT	VIT A	VIT C	CALCIUM	IRON	F.ACID	FIBRE
gm	kcal	gm	gm	gm	mcg	mg	mg	mg	mcg	gm
132	114	3.0	16.9	4.0	280.3	24.3	64.1	1.1	31.7	0.9

Broccoli Broth

A really quick soup to make and one which does not require you to hunt for lots of ingredients to whip it up.

Broccoli is one of the best sources of folic acid. I have added this simple soup to provide for lots of folic acid in your diet which you will need in plenty during your first trimester and more importantly before you conceive. It is also rich in calcium and protein.

Prep. time : 15 min.   Cooking time : 15 min.   Serves 2.

1 cup broccoli, chopped
½ cup onion, chopped
1 teaspoon wheat germ
1 tablespoon cheese
½ cup milk
1 teaspoon oil
salt and pepper to taste

1. Heat the oil, add the onion and sauté till the pieces are translucent.
2. Add the chopped broccoli and 1½ cups of water and simmer for 2 to 3 minutes. Cool.
3. Purée in a liquidiser and transfer back into a pan.
4. Add the milk, wheat germ and cheese and bring to a boil.
5. Add salt and pepper and serve hot.

Handy tip

Wheat germ is the outer covering of the wheat grain and is extremely rich in fibre. Readymade wheat germ is available in packets at most health food stores. If you cannot find wheat germ, this soup will taste just as good without it.

Nutritive values per serving :

AMT	ENERGY	PROTEIN	CHO	FAT	VIT A	VIT C	CALCIUM	IRON	F.ACID	FIBRE
gm	kcal	gm	gm	gm	mcg	mg	mg	mg	mcg	gm
11.7	124	4.7	8.1	7.1	764.8	27.5	179.3	0.7	21.8	0.6

Healthy Tomato Soup

The ever popular tomato soup made healthier with the addition of moong dal. Tomatoes are rich in folic acid, vitamin C and moong dal provides protein.
Moong dal also cuts down the sharpness of tomatoes and gives this soup a velvety texture. Just pour it into your favourite mug and sip away....

Prep. time : 5 min.   Cooking time : 25 min.   Serves 6.

5 cups chopped tomatoes
⅓ cup yellow moong dal (split yellow gram), washed
1 onion, finely chopped
1 tablespoon cornflour or plain flour (maida)
1 to 2 teaspoons sugar (if required)
⅓ cup warm milk
2 teaspoons butter
salt and pepper to taste

For serving (optional)
fresh cream
bread croutons

1. Pressure cook the tomatoes with the moong dal in 3 to 4 cups of water till the dal is cooked.
2. Cool and blend in a liquidiser. Keep aside.
3. Melt the butter, add the onion, sauté for 3 to 4 minutes and add the puréed mixture.
4. Mix the cornflour with a little water and pour into the soup. Simmer for 2 minutes, stirring occasionally.
5. Add the sugar, milk, salt and pepper and bring to a boil. Serve hot garnished with cream and bread croutons.

Nutritive values per serving :

AMT	ENERGY	PROTEIN	CHO	FAT	VIT A	VIT C	CALCIUM	IRON	F.ACID	FIBRE
gm	kcal	gm	gm	gm	mcg	mg	mg	mg	mcg	gm
166	87	3.9	12.9	1.9	510.7	36.7	98.5	1.3	52.3	1.2

Potato and Carrot Soup

The versatile potato often plays a supporting role in a meal, but in this recipe it's the star in creating a creamy soup that is brightened up with the addition of grated carrots.

Try not to peel the potatoes when you cook and purée them because unpeeled potatoes are rich in folic acid.

Carbohydrates tend to be the best tolerated nutrient in early pregnancy, so this soup is a boon for those days.

Picture on page 101

Prep. time : 10 min.   Cooking time : 15 min.   Serves 2.

1 cup potatoes, diced (preferably with the peel on)
¼ cup onion, sliced
½ teaspoon mixed dried herbs (oregano, thyme etc.)
1 teaspoon butter
salt and pepper to taste

For the garnish
carrot, grated

1. Melt the butter in a pressure cooker, sauté the onion for a while.
2. Add the potatoes and sauté for a few more minutes.
3. Then add 1½ cups of water and pressure cook for 3 whistles. Cool completely.
4. Blend in a liquidiser and add the mixed herbs, salt and pepper.
5. Reheat the soup and serve garnished with grated carrots.

Nutritive values per serving :

AMT	ENERGY	PROTEIN	CHO	FAT	VIT A	VIT C	CALCIUM	IRON	F.ACID	FIBRE
gm	kcal	gm	gm	gm	mcg	mg	mg	mg	mcg	gm
66	65	0.9	12.4	1.3	266.9	9.0	16.9	0.4	5.3	0.4

Spinach and Paneer Soup

Another simple soup that is really quick to make and provides a whole lot of nutrients. Spinach is rich in folic acid, iron and fibre and paneer in protein, calcium and energy.
I have kept the flavours simple, keeping in mind your delicate palate during the first trimester, but if you can handle mild flavours, add a little garlic (approximately 1 to 2 cloves) or about ¼ teaspoon of mixed dried herbs to "pep" up this soup.

Prep. time : 10 min.   Cooking time : 10 min.   Serves 4.

2½ cups spinach (palak), chopped
½ cup paneer (cottage chesse), crumbled
½ cup onion, chopped
1 teaspoon oil
salt to taste

1. Heat the oil and sauté the onion for 2 to 3 minutes.
2. Add the spinach and sauté for another 4 to 5 minutes. Cool slightly.
3. Blend the onion and spinach mixture with 4 cups of water in a blender till it is a smooth purée.
4. Add the crumbled paneer and salt to the purée and bring it to a boil.
   Serve hot.

Nutritive values per serving :

AMT	ENERGY	PROTEIN	CHO	FAT	VIT A	VIT C	CALCIUM	IRON	F.ACID	FIBRE
gm	kcal	gm	gm	gm	mcg	mg	mg	mg	mcg	gm
82	90	3.6	8.3	4.7	2441.0	14.3	130.0	0.6	53.3	0.4

Golden Broth

This is one of my all-time favourite soup recipes which is also very nutritive as it is rich in Vitamin A, fibre and protein. Instead of fried starters, this "sunny" soup is just perfect as a pre-dinner appetizer.

Prep. time : 15 min.   Cooking time : 20 min.   Serves 4.

For the stock
2 large carrots, chopped
2 onions, chopped
1 potato, chopped

For the topping
½ onion, chopped
¾ cup chopped spinach (palak)
¾ cup milk
1 tablespoon butter
salt and pepper to taste

For the stock
1. Combine all the ingredients, add 5 cups of water and pressure cook for 2 to 3 whistles.
2. When cooked, blend in a liquidiser and keep aside.

For the topping
1. Heat the butter and sauté the onion for 1 minute.
2. Add the spinach and sauté again for a little while.
3. Add the stock and boil for a few minutes.
4. Warm the milk and add it to the soup. Add salt and pepper.
Serve hot.

Nutritive values per serving :

AMT	ENERGY	PROTEIN	CHO	FAT	VIT A	VIT C	CALCIUM	IRON	F.ACID	FIBRE
gm	kcal	gm	gm	gm	mcg	mg	mg	mg	mcg	gm
176	136	3.3	17.7	4.9	1808.6	14.5	156.0	1.2	29.9	1.1

Bean Soup

A rich soup that is low in calories but high in carbohydrates, fibre and iron. Puréed beans give this soup a smooth rich consistency without the addition of thickeners like flour, milk, cream etc.

This satisfying soup will agree well with you even if you are suffering from nausea.

Prep. time : 10 min.   Cooking time : 15 min.   Serves 4.

¾ cup red kidney beans (rajma)
2 onions, chopped
4 tomatoes, chopped
3 cloves garlic, chopped
½ teaspoon chilli powder
1 teaspoon lemon juice
1 tablespoon oil
salt to taste

For serving
finely chopped tomatoes
sliced spring onions
chopped coriander
Tabasco sauce

1. Soak the beans overnight. Drain thoroughly.
2. Heat the oil, add the onions and fry for 1 minute. Add the tomatoes, garlic, chilli powder and salt and sauté for 1 more minute.
3. Add the beans and 6 cups of water and pressure cook till they are soft. Blend in a blender.
4. Do not strain. Add the lemon juice and mix well. Serve hot topped with tomatoes, onions, coriander and Tabasco sauce.

Nutritive values per serving :

AMT	ENERGY	PROTEIN	CHO	FAT	VIT A	VIT C	CALCIUM	IRON	F.ACID	FIBRE
gm	kcal	gm	gm	gm	mcg	mg	mg	mg	mcg	gm
152	168	7.7	24.6	4.3	307.5	26.4	131.2	2.2	25.8	2.3

Winter Vegetable Soup

This hearty lentil based soup has warm flavours making it very appealing throughout your pregnancy. The potatoes and beans add extra carbohydrates while the vegetables provide the required vitamins, minerals and fibre.
It is a great one dish meal when you are lactating too. Simply assemble everything in a pot and let it simmer away while you attend to your little one.

Prep. time : 20 min.   Cooking time : 1 hour.   Serves 6.

3 tablespoons black-eyed beans (chawli)
⅓ cup french beans, chopped
⅓ cup carrot, cubed
⅓ cup potato, cubed
⅓ cup cauliflower florets
⅓ cup tomato cubes, without seeds
¾ cup shredded cabbage
1 onion, chopped
2 tablespoons celery stalks, chopped
2 bay leaves
1 tablespoon butter
salt and pepper to taste

For the garnish
2 tablespoons chopped parsley
2 tablespoons grated cheese

1. Soak the black-eyed beans in water for 3 to 4 hours. Drain and keep aside.
2. Heat the butter in a pan and sauté the onion, celery and bay leaves lightly. Add the french beans, carrots, potatoes and cauliflower and cook for 5 to 7 minutes.
3. Add 6 cups of water and simmer on a medium flame for 30 to 45 minutes until the beans are tender.
4. Add the cabbage and tomato and simmer for 3 to 4 minutes.

5. Add salt and pepper.
   Serve hot, garnished with the chopped parsley and grated cheese.

Handy tip Chawli beans are also called haricot beans or lobhia beans and are available at most grocery stores.

Nutritive values per serving :

AMT	ENERGY	PROTEIN	CHO	FAT	VIT A	VIT C	CALCIUM	IRON	F.ACID	FIBRE
gm	kcal	gm	gm	gm	mcg	mg	mg	mg	mcg	gm
47	57	2.7	7.8	1.7	220.9	12.8	34.6	0.8	7.2	0.8

Salads

Three Bean Salad

This salad is an excellent source of folic acid. Enjoy it during your preconception period and also your first trimester, as it also a good source of iron and protein.

Prep. time : 10 min.   No cooking.   Serves 4.

2½ cups mixed boiled beans (rajma, chawli, kabuli chana, hara chana)
⅔ cup spring onions, sliced
½ cup tomato, diced
1 to 2 green chillies, finely chopped
2 tablespoons chopped coriander

To be mixed into a dressing
2 tablespoons lemon juice
2 teaspoons chaat masala
¼ teaspoon black salt (sanchal)
salt and pepper to taste

1. Keeping aside half the coriander leaves for the garnish and mix all the salad ingredients together.
2. Toss in the dressing and refrigerate for at least for 1 hour. Serve cold, garnished with the balance coriander leaves.

Nutritive values per serving :

AMT	ENERGY	PROTEIN	CHO	FAT	VIT A	VIT C	CALCIUM	IRON	F.ACID	FIBRE
gm	kcal	gm	gm	gm	mcg	mg	mg	mg	mcg	gm
73	147	8.7	25.7	1.0	180.0	9.8	79.9	2.7	38.5	2.0

Sweet Corn and Kidney Bean Salad

This salad is an excellent choice for a working lunch as it keeps well for sometime without refrigeration.
Packed with fibre, iron and carbohydrates it will keep you "full" for a few hours. The innovative dressing is flavourful without being loaded with oil.

Prep. time : a few min.   Cooking time : 10 min.   Serves 4.

1½ cups cooked kidney beans (rajma)
1½ cups cooked fresh corn (preferably sweet corn)
1 small onion, chopped
salt and pepper to taste

For the dressing
2 teaspoons cornflour
1 tablespoon onion, finely chopped
2 tablespoons vinegar
2 tablespoons tomato ketchup
2 tablespoons vegetable oil
½ teaspoon sugar
½ teaspoon prepared mustard
¼ teaspoon chilli powder
1 clove garlic, crushed (optional)
½ teaspoon Worcestershire sauce
½ teaspoon salt

For the dressing
1. Mix the cornflour with ¾ cup of water in a saucepan and cook over medium heat until the mixture is clear and thick. Cool.
2. Add the remaining ingredients, put in a jar and shake well. Keep aside till required.

How to proceed
1. Combine all the salad ingredients in a bowl and refrigerate.
2. Just before serving, add the dressing as required and toss.
   Serve cold.

This dressing can be refrigerated and kept till the next time you make this salad again (approx. 10 days).

Nutritive values per serving :

AMT	ENERGY	PROTEIN	CHO	FAT	VIT A	VIT C	CALCIUM	IRON	F.ACID	FIBRE
gm	kcal	gm	gm	gm	mcg	mg	mg	mg	mcg	gm
102	241	6.7	35.7	8.2	177.1	11.1	70.9	1.9	3.1	1.4

Energy Salad

This salad is a good source of iron, vitamin C, potassium and fructose which is a source of instant energy. It will perk you up almost instantly.
It makes a great snack that can be assembled quickly at any time using all your favourite fruits.

Prep. time : 10 min.   Cooking time : 10 min.   Serves 4.

1½ cups cauliflower florets
4 dates (khajur), chopped
1 banana, sliced
1 orange, segmented
2 unpeeled red apples, cut into cubes
juice of ½ lemon
½ teaspoon grated lemon rind
½ tablespoon oil
½ tablespoon vinegar
salt and pepper to taste

For the orange dressing
⅓ cup thick fresh curds (yoghurt)
4 teaspoons orange juice
½ teaspoon mustard powder
½ teaspoon powdered sugar
a pinch salt

1. For the orange dressing, whisk all the ingredients together and chill.
2. Steam the cauliflower florets for 5 minutes. Cool.

3. Combine the oil, vinegar, salt and pepper. Marinate the cauliflower in this mixture for at least 1 hour.
4. Combine all the other ingredients in the bowl and chill. Serve chilled with the orange dressing.

Nutritive values per serving :

AMT	ENERGY	PROTEIN	CHO	FAT	VIT A	VIT C	CALCIUM	IRON	F.ACID	FIBRE
gm	kcal	gm	gm	gm	mcg	mg	mg	mg	mcg	gm
216	151	2.4	25.6	3.9	362.4	34.8	74.1	1.4	1.1	1.8

Fruity Bean Salad

I often create new recipes with what is left in the refrigerator. Many of these creations work and my family lets me know when they don't. This is one of those recipes that got a hearty nod. It provides adequate amounts of calcium, vitamin C and fibre. Sprouting the pulses increases their nutrient content and also makes them easier to digest as compared to whole unsprouted pulses.

Prep. time : 20 min.   Cooking time : 30 min.   Serves 8.

1½ cups mixed sprouted pulses (math, chick peas, moong etc.), boiled
¾ cup apples, chopped
segments of 1 orange
2 tablespoons grapes, halved
2 tablespoons sliced white radish
¾ cup chopped salad leaves
½ cup chopped spinach leaves
1 finely chopped green chilli (optional)
salt to taste

To be mixed into a dressing
¾ cup fresh curds (yoghurt)
2 tablespoons chopped mint leaves
1 teaspoon sugar
salt to taste

1. Mix all the ingredients except the dressing thoroughly and put to chill.
2. Just before serving, pour the dressing over the salad. Serve chilled.

Handy tip   Wash all the greens thoroughly before using them in your salad. Dry all the washed greens on a tissue or a dry kitchen towel before adding the dressing.

Nutritive values per serving :

AMT	ENERGY	PROTEIN	CHO	FAT	VIT A	VIT C	CALCIUM	IRON	F.ACID	FIBRE
gm	kcal	gm	gm	gm	mcg	mg	mg	mg	mcg	gm
141	161	7.1	23.5	3.4	1009.6	13.6	146.6	2.4	32.5	1.5

Orange Sesame Tabbouleh

A *delightful orange sesame flavoured bulgur wheat salad.*
This salad is soothing, especially if you are feeling nauseous
and don't feel like eating much. Broken wheat is a good source
of carbohydrates which will help you feel better and also
nourish you with iron, vitamin C and fibre.
This dish combines bulgur wheat with onions, tomatoes and
parsley with orange squash, olive oil and lemon juice, all of
which provide contrasting flavours and textures that will
surely appeal to you.

Prep. time : 15 min.   Cooking time : 10 min.   Serves 4.

1 cup bulgur wheat (dalia)
1 tablespoon grated orange zest
2 tablespoons toasted sesame (til) seeds
2 spring onions, chopped
1 tomato, diced
½ cup parsley, finely chopped
2 tablespoons lemon juice
2 tablespoons olive oil
2 tablespoons orange squash
salt to taste

1. Cook the bulgur wheat in 1½ cups of water for 10 minutes till it is tender.
2. Drain and pour cold water over to cool the bulgur wheat.
3. Drain again and keep aside.
4. Combine all the ingredients in a bowl and mix well.
5. Refrigerate for at least 1 hour before serving so that all the flavours blend.

Handy tip

While grating the orange zest, be careful not to be grate the white pith, as it is bitter.

Nutritive values per serving :

AMT	ENERGY	PROTEIN	CHO	FAT	VIT A	VIT C	CALCIUM	IRON	F.ACID	FIBRE
gm	kcal	gm	gm	gm	mcg	mg	mg	mg	mcg	gm
106	250	4.6	34.5	10.5	171.7	16.3	119.3	2.8	13.4	1.5

Stir Fry Salad

Picture on page 76

A colourful assortment of vegetables tossed lightly with cottage cheese and onion seeds.

This recipe is a delicious source of fibre, iron, vitamin A, vitamin C and calcium. If you are one of those who prefers eating hot vegetables dishes to cold salads, then this is just the one for you. Have the salad with hot garlic bread or toss some pasta in it to make it more filling.

Prep. time : 10 min.   Cooking time : 5 min.   Serves 4.

1 cup capsicum, cut into thin strips
1 cup paneer (cottage cheese), cut into tin strips
1 spring onion, sliced
½ cup baby corn, sliced
½ cucumber, sliced
½ cup broccoli florets
¼ cup bean sprouts
1 small tomato, deseeded and sliced
1 teaspoon onion seeds (kalonji)
1 teaspoon oil
salt to taste

1. Heat the oil and add the onion seeds.
2. Add all the vegetables and salt and sauté on a high flame till the vegetables are tender.
3. Add the paneer and sauté for another minute.
4. Remove from the flame and serve immediately.

Handy tip

You can add 3 colours of capsicum (yellow, red and green) as shown in the picture on page 76.

Nutritive values per serving :

AMT	ENERGY	PROTEIN	CHO	FAT	VIT A	VIT C	CALCIUM	IRON	F.ACID	FIBRE
gm	kcal	gm	gm	gm	mcg	mg	mg	mg	mcg	gm
136	172	7.6	12.3	10.4	517.6	56.8	210.9	1.1	12.0	1.0

Chick Pea Salad

One of the most nutritious of all beans, chick peas (or garbanzo beans) are rich in iron, protein and folic acid. Curds and paneer enrich this tangy salad with more protein and also calcium, while coriander and mint increase its vitamin A content.
Chill this salad thoroughly before you eat it.

Prep. time : 15 min.   Cooking time : 20 min.   Serves 2.

½ cup chick peas (kabuli chana), soaked overnight
1 firm tomato, cubed
2 spring onions, sliced
½ cup paneer (cottage cheese), diced
½ cup cucumber, diced

For the curd dressing
½ cup chopped mint leaves
¼ cup chopped coriander
a small piece of ginger
½ green chilli
3 tablespoons fresh curds (yoghurt)
salt to taste

For the dressing
Combine all the ingredients and blend into a smooth purée. Refrigerate.

For the salad
1. Drain and wash the soaked chick peas. Add fresh water and salt and pressure cook for 3 to 4 whistles till they are soft. Cool completely.
2. Combine with the remaining ingredients for the salad.
3. Add the dressing and mix well.
   Serve chilled.

Nutritive values per serving :

AMT	ENERGY	PROTEIN	CHO	FAT	VIT A	VIT C	CALCIUM	IRON	F.ACID	FIBRE
gm	kcal	gm	gm	gm	mcg	mg	mg	mg	mcg	gm
192	240	10.7	23.2	11.0	672.4	24.4	320.7	2.8	65.7	1.6

Tossed Salad

A simple salad made with ingredients that are usually handy in every kitchen. The dressing is what makes this salad so special. Its simple refreshing flavours complement those of the salad ingredients (i.e. the tomato, lettuce, cucumber and cheese) perfectly.

What I usually do is make a large quantity of this dressing and refrigerate it, so I don't have to keep making a dressing each time I make the salad. Also, the flavours mellow better if they are left together for a while.

This recipe will nourish you with calcium and protein from the cheese and provide vitamin C from the lemon juice which will also help in the absorption of iron.

Prep. time : 10 min.   No cooking.   Serves 4.

¾ cup tomato, cubed
1 cup cucumber, cubed
1½ cups lettuce, torn
½ cup cheese, cubed

To be mixed into a dressing
2 tablespoons lemon juice
2 tablespoons olive oil or salad oil
1 large clove garlic, finely chopped
salt and pepper to taste

1. Combine all the ingredients for the salad and chill till required.
2. Before serving, add the dressing and toss the salad. Serve immediately.

If you want to take this salad for lunch to the office, add the salt just before you sit down to eat. Do not add it in the dressing beforehand, as all the vegetables will soften on adding salt.

Nutritive values per serving :

AMT	ENERGY	PROTEIN	CHO	FAT	VIT A	VIT C	CALCIUM	IRON	F.ACID	FIBRE
gm	kcal	gm	gm	gm	mcg	mg	mg	mg	mcg	gm
162	166	6.4	6.2	12.7	816.7	21.9	209.7	2.3	13.3	0.9

Fruit and Lettuce Salad

Picture on facing page

This is one of my favourite dishes for a summer lunch. Fresh fruits are tossed with salad greens and then dressed in a syrupy sweet and spicy dressing that is inspired by a Thai salad.
This salad is a visual delight that is rich in iron, fibre, vitamin C and fructose.

Prep. time : 15 min.   Cooking time : 10 min.   Serves 4.

1 cup assorted lettuce, shredded (iceberg, curly, red lettuce etc.)
½ cup papaya, diced
½ cup grapes, halved
½ cup orange segments
½ cup guava, sliced

1) Potato and Carrot Soup, *page 85*
2) Fruit and Lettuce Salad, *facing page*

½ cup strawberries, quartered
½ cup watermelon, diced
1 tablespoon sliced almonds, toasted

For the dressing
2 tablespoons vinegar
¾ cup sugar
1 cup water
1 tablespoon red chilli flakes (paprika)
1 tablespoon salt

1. Combine the fruits and lettuce in a large bowl and chill.
2. For the dressing, combine the vinegar, sugar and water and boil to make a thick syrup.
3. Cool slightly and add the red chilli flakes and salt and mix well.
4. Cool completely and store in a sterilised air-tight bottle.
5. Just before serving, pour some of the dressing over the salad and toss.

Handy tip

You can use any seasonal fruits of your choice in case any of the above fruits is not in season.

Nutritive values per serving :

AMT	ENERGY	PROTEIN	CHO	FAT	VIT A	VIT C	CALCIUM	IRON	F.ACID	FIBRE
gm	kcal	gm	gm	gm	mcg	mg	mg	mg	mcg	gm
139	183	2.1	37.8	2.5	758.8	30.7	48.6	3.3	0.0	1.2

1) Pineapple Crumble, *page 146*
2) High Fibre Bread, *page 71*
3) Easy Cheesy Vegetable Pasta, *page 142*

Cabbage and Moong Dal Salad

Rich in protein, fibre and iron, this simple salad is good for a mid morning or a late afternoon snack. It will tickle your taste buds and satisfy your hunger pangs without giving you any empty calories.

You can have it for lunch as a side dish or take it to work as this salad holds well without refrigeration for a couple of hours.

Prep. time : 10 min.   Cooking time : 5 min.   Serves 4.

2 cups cabbage, chopped
⅓ cup yellow moong dal (split yellow gram), soaked for 2 to 3 hours
½ teaspoon mustard seeds (rai)
2 to 3 curry leaves
¼ teaspoon asafoetida (hing)
1 green chilli, chopped
3 tablespoons chopped coriander
1 tablespoon grated coconut
1 teaspoon sugar (optional)
1 teaspoon lemon juice
salt to taste

1. Wash and drain the soaked moong dal. Keep aside.
2. Heat the oil and add the mustard seeds. When they crackle, add the curry leaves, asafoetida and green chilli and stir.
3. Add the cabbage, moong dal and salt. Sauté over a high flame for 2 to 3 minutes, till the dal softens a little.
4. Transfer into a bowl and when it cools slightly, add the coriander, coconut, sugar and lemon juice and mix well.
5. Serve chilled or at room temperature.

Nutritive values per serving :

AMT	ENERGY	PROTEIN	CHO	FAT	VIT A	VIT C	CALCIUM	IRON	F.ACID	FIBRE
gm	kcal	gm	gm	gm	mcg	mg	mg	mg	mcg	gm
63	75	4.1	11.5	1.4	211.1	54.9	31.7	0.9	27.6	0.7

Dals and Vegetables

Hariyali Dal

A tasty dal, made with masoor dal and greens. Spinach and fenugreek leaves are a good source of vitamin A, iron and calcium. All dals are rich sources of protein and energy. Masoor dal is easier to digest than arhar dal. It is therefore a better choice for you when you're pregnant, as it will provide you with protein and yet not leave you feeling uncomfortable after you have eaten.

This dal is a slightly dry preparation and if you want to have it with rice, you may need to add a little more water to "thin" it down.

Prep. time : 10 min.   Cooking time : 20 min.   Serves 6 to 8.

1 cup uncooked masoor dal (split red lentils)
2 cups greens (palak, methi, coriander)
1 onion, chopped
1 teaspoon cumin seeds (jeera)
2 teaspoons amchur (dry mango powder)
1 tomato, chopped
1/2 teaspoon turmeric powder (haldi)
3/4 teaspoon chilli powder
1 tablespoon ghee
salt to taste

To be ground into a paste
6 cloves garlic
4 to 6 green chillies
25 mm. (1") piece ginger

1. Cook the dal separately with 2 cups of water in a pressure cooker.
2. Heat the ghee in a pan, add the onion and cumin seeds and sauté for at least 2 minutes.
3. Add the cooked dal, the greens, amchur, tomato,

turmeric powder, chilli powder, paste and salt and cook for a few minutes.

Serve hot.

Nutritive values per serving :

AMT	ENERGY	PROTEIN	CHO	FAT	VIT A	VIT C	CALCIUM	IRON	F.ACID	FIBRE
gm	kcal	gm	gm	gm	mcg	mg	mg	mg	mcg	gm
57	29	0.5	2.1	2.0	645.9	10.7	29.1	0.3	11.9	0.3

Soya Mutter ki Subzi

Soyabean nuggets and green peas simmered in a tangy gravy. Soyabean nuggets are processed from soyabeans to make them more digestible and palatable. They are a very rich source of vegetarian protein and Vitamin B12. This subzi is good for your preconception period and also throughout your pregnancy as the energy, protein and vitamin A content of the recipe are good.

Prep. time : 10 min.   Cooking time : 40 min.   Serves 2.

$\frac{1}{2}$ cup soya nuggets
$\frac{1}{2}$ cup green peas, boiled
$\frac{1}{2}$ teaspoon cumin seeds (jeera)
a pinch asafoetida (hing)
1 teaspoon ginger-green chilli paste
$\frac{1}{2}$ teaspoon garlic paste
2 medium onions, chopped
2 tomatoes, finely chopped
$\frac{1}{4}$ teaspoon turmeric powder (haldi)
$\frac{1}{2}$ teaspoon chilli powder
$\frac{1}{2}$ teaspoon coriander (dhania) powder
$\frac{1}{4}$ cup fresh curds (yoghurt)
2 teaspoons Bengal gram flour (besan)
2 tablespoons milk
$\frac{1}{2}$ teaspoon sugar
1 teaspoon oil
salt to taste

1. Cook the soya nuggets in hot salted water for about 20 minutes. Drain and keep aside.
2. Heat the oil and add the cumin seeds. When they crackle, add the asafoetida, ginger-green chilli paste, garlic paste and onions and sauté till the onions are translucent. Add a tablespoon of water if you find the masala burning.
3. Add the tomatoes, turmeric powder, chilli powder and coriander powder and cook on a slow flame for about 5 to 10 minutes.
4. Mix the curds, gram flour, milk and ¾ cup of water and add to the onion-tomato gravy.
5. Add the soya nuggets, green peas, sugar and salt and simmer for 2 more minutes.
Serve hot.

Handy tip

You can use mushrooms or paneer instead of the soya nuggets as a variation.

Nutritive values per serving :

AMT	ENERGY	PROTEIN	CHO	FAT	VIT A	VIT C	CALCIUM	IRON	F.ACID	FIBRE
gm	kcal	gm	gm	gm	mcg	mg	mg	mg	mcg	gm
298	286	14.2	27.0	11.3	528.6	33.4	301.5	3.2	53.5	3.0

Broccoli Aloo aur Paneer ki Subzi

Picture on page 127

A simple vegetable stir fry with an unusual combination of vegetables. Broccoli is a very good source of folic acid and fibre, potatoes provide carbohydrates and paneer contributes calcium and protein to this dish.
Try this garlic flavoured stir fry with hot phulkas. I guarantee that you will love it.

Prep. time : 10 min.   Cooking time : 15 min.   Serves 4.

½ cup Madras onions, peeled
1 cup potato, diced unpeeled
1 cup broccoli florets
½ cup paneer (cottage cheese), cut into strips

1 teaspoon ginger-garlic paste
1 teaspoon chilli flakes (paprika)
1 teaspoon oil
salt to taste
6 to 8 cherry tomatoes (optional)

1. Heat the oil, add the ginger-garlic paste and onions and sauté for a few minutes.
2. Add the potato and salt and sauté for another 4 to 5 minutes.
3. Add 2 to 3 tablespoons of water and the broccoli and cook till the potatoes are done.
4. Add the paneer and chilli flakes, mix well and sauté for 4 to 5 minutes.
   Serve hot.

Nutritive values per serving :

AMT	ENERGY	PROTEIN	CHO	FAT	VIT A	VIT C	CALCIUM	IRON	F.ACID	FIBRE
gm	kcal	gm	gm	gm	mcg	mg	mg	mg	mcg	gm
68	98	3.4	8.6	5.6	410.4	17.5	109.4	0.3	9.6	0.8

Dahi Chane ki Subzi

Curds are a very good source of calcium and are also very easy to digest. Pulses along with curds improve the protein and calcium content of this recipe. Fibre and iron are also well represented. Your energy requirements are high during the second trimester and this recipe provides sufficient energy in your diet.

Prep. time : 15 min.   Cooking time : 15 min.   Serves 4.

1 cup red chana (whole red gram), soaked overnight
½ teaspoon cumin seeds (jeera)
¼ teaspoon mustard seeds (rai)
2 bay leaves
4 whole red chillies
⅛ teaspoon asafoetida (hing)
1 teaspoon ginger-green chilli paste
1 teaspoon chilli powder

1 teaspoon chilli powder
¼ teaspoon turmeric powder (haldi)
1 cup curds (yoghurt)
2 teaspoons Bengal gram flour (besan)
4 tablespoons chopped coriander
1 tablespoon oil
salt to taste

1. Heat the oil in a pressure cooker, add the cumin seeds, mustard seeds, bay leaves, red chilies and asafoetida. When the seeds crackle, add the red chana, ginger-green chilli paste, chilli powder, turmeric powder and salt with 2 cups of water. Pressure cook for 2 to 3 whistles till the chana is cooked.
2. Whisk the curds and gram flour together and add the mixture to the cooked chana. Bring to a boil and simmer for 4 to 5 minutes. Stir this continuously till the mixture comes to a boil since the curds can split if they are not stirred. Serve hot garnished with the coriander.

Handy tip You can also substitute the chana with lobhia beans (chawli).

Nutritive values per serving:

AMT	ENERGY	PROTEIN	CHO	FAT	VIT A	VIT C	CALCIUM	IRON	F.ACID	FIBRE
gm	kcal	gm	gm	gm	mcg	mg	mg	mg	mcg	gm
75	118	4.2	7.0	10.3	399.4	8.6	120.6	0.4	5.0	0.7

Usli

Picture on cover page

Usli consists of a mixture of healthy sprouts that are stir fried with a little masala.

A combination of 3 sprouts makes the recipe a good source of protein and iron. Sprouting aids the digestion of these pulses and also increases their nutritive value. The calcium and the fibre content of the recipe is good. It is thus very beneficial for you and also keeps your taste buds happy.

Prep. time : 10 min.   Cooking time : 10 min.   Serves 4.

2 cups mixed sprouts (moong, chana, matki etc.)
1 teaspoon cumin seeds (jeera)
1 onion, chopped
$\frac{1}{2}$ teaspoon ginger, chopped
4 cloves garlic, chopped
2 green chillies, chopped
1 tomato, chopped
$\frac{1}{4}$ teaspoon turmeric powder (haldi)
1 tablespoon chopped coriander
$\frac{1}{2}$ teaspoon chilli powder
1 teaspoon lemon juice
2 tablespoons oil
salt to taste

1. Parboil the sprouts and drain. Do not cook them in a pressure cooker.
2. Heat the oil in a pan, add the cumin seeds and fry for $\frac{1}{2}$ minute. Add the onion and fry for a few seconds.
3. Add the ginger, garlic and green chillies and fry again for a few seconds.
4. Add the tomato, turmeric powder, coriander and chilli powder and fry again.
5. Add the drained sprouts, lemon juice and salt and mix well. Serve hot.

Nutritive values per serving :

AMT	ENERGY	PROTEIN	CHO	FAT	VIT A	VIT C	CALCIUM	IRON	F.ACID	FIBRE
gm	kcal	gm	gm	gm	mcg	mg	mg	mg	mcg	gm
91	263	9.8	21.8	15.1	220.9	9.9	80.8	2.1	30.0	1.9

Sai Bhaji

This traditional Sindhi recipe is a good combination of leafy vegetables with dal which provides plenty of iron, calcium and vitamin A. The energy, protein and fibre levels are high due to addition of dal along with the vegetables.
Relish it with steamed rice or any kind of roti.

Prep. time : 10 min.   Cooking time : 25 min.   Serves 2.

3 tablespoons split Bengal gram (chana dal)
3 cups spinach (palak), chopped
¾ cup khatta bhaji (khatta palak)
½ teaspoon cumin seeds (jeera)
1 onion, chopped
1 potato, chopped
2 small brinjals, chopped
2 teaspoons ginger-garlic paste
1 teaspoon chilli powder
2 teaspoon coriander (dhania) powder
a pinch turmeric powder (haldi)
2 tablespoons oil
salt to taste

1. Combine the chana dal with 1 cup of water and pressure cook for 1 whistle. Drain the excess water and keep aside.
2. Heat the oil in a pressure cooker and add the cumin seeds.
3. When the seeds crackle, add the onion, potato, brinjals and ginger-garlic paste and sauté for 5 to 7 minutes.
4. Add the chilli powder, coriander powder, turmeric powder and salt and sauté for 2 to 3 minutes.

5. Add the spinach, khatta bhaji and the cooked chana dal and pressure cook for 2 whistles.
6. Allow to cool and whisk the mixture well.
   Serve hot.

Handy tip

Khatta bhaji is available at most vegetable vendors. It looks like a smaller version of spinach leaves and the leaves are slightly sour in taste.

Nutritive values per serving :

AMT	ENERGY	PROTEIN	CHO	FAT	VIT A	VIT C	CALCIUM	IRON	F.ACID	FIBRE
gm	kcal	gm	gm	gm	mcg	mg	mg	mg	mcg	gm
267	314	8.8	30.9	17.3	6818.4	45.2	130.6	3.1	206.4	1.8

Paatal Bhaji (colocasia ambti)

Your calcium requirement shoots up during the third trimester and so it is necessary to have foods that can meet these requirements. This dish is an excellent source of iron, calcium and fibre.

Prep. time : 10 min.   Cooking time : 20 min.   Serves 4.

5 cups colocasia leaves with stems (patra leaves, alu che paan), chopped
¼ cup chana dal (split Bengal gram), soaked
2 teaspoons jaggery (gur)
1 tablespoon tamarind pulp
1 tablespoon roasted peanuts, crushed
1 tablespoon Bengal gram flour (besan), dissolved in 2 tablespoons of water
a pinch asafoetida (hing)
½ teaspoon turmeric powder (haldi)
1 teaspoon oil
salt to taste

To be ground into a paste

½ cup grated coconut

3 green chillies

½ cup chopped coriander

6 mm. (¼") piece ginger

For the tempering

1 teaspoon oil

½ teaspoon mustard seeds (rai)

½ teaspoon cumin seeds (jeera)

a pinch asafoetida (hing)

1. Heat the oil, add the asafoetida, chopped colocasia leaves with stems, soaked chana dal and peanuts and sauté for 2 minutes.
2. Add the turmeric powder, tamarind pulp, 1 cup of water, jaggery and salt and cook till the chana dal is cooked.
3. Add the ground paste and the besan paste and cook till the mixture thickens.
4. For the tempering, heat the oil in a small pan and add the mustard seeds. When they crackle, add the cumin seeds and asafoetida.
5. Pour the tempering mixture over the cooked vegetable and mix well.
   Serve hot.

Nutritive values per serving :

AMT	ENERGY	PROTEIN	CHO	FAT	VIT A	VIT C	CALCIUM	IRON	F.ACID	FIBRE
gm	kcal	gm	gm	gm	mcg	mg	mg	mg	mcg	gm
93	185	6.2	16.6	10.4	6027.2	11.0	146.0	6.7	19.6	2.4

Subzi Dal

Have this nutritious dal along with rotis or parathas as the combination of dals with vegetables makes it extremely rich in energy, protein, calcium, iron and folic acid — all the nutrients which are necessary for a successful pregnancy. Green peas add on to the fibre content of the recipe and help to relieve constipation. Also, coriander and capsicum are an important source of vitamins A and C.

Prep. time : 15 min.   Cooking time : 30 min.   Serves 4.

⅓ cup yellow moong dal (split yellow gram)
⅓ cup toovar (arhar) dal
⅓ cup masoor dal (split red lentils)
½ teaspoon mustard seeds (rai)
½ teaspoon cumin seeds (jeera)
6 to 8 curry leaves
¼ teaspoon asafoetida (hing)
1 green chilli, chopped
1 onion, chopped
2 teaspoons ginger-green chilli paste
½ teaspoon garlic paste
1 large tomato, finely chopped
½ teaspoon chilli powder
½ teaspoon turmeric powder (haldi)
1 cup mixed vegetables (capsicum, carrots, peas), finely chopped
1 tablespoon oil
salt to taste

For the garnish
2 tablespoons chopped coriander

1. Wash and pressure cook the dals together with 2 cups of water till the dals are cooked. Keep aside.
2. Heat the oil in a pan and add the mustard seeds and cumin seeds. When they crackle, add the curry leaves and asafoetida.
3. Add the green chilli and onion and sauté for 3 to 4 minutes.

4. Add the ginger-green chilli paste, garlic paste and tomato and sauté for 3 to 4 more minutes.
5. Add the chilli powder, turmeric powder and mixed vegetables and mix well.
6. Add the dals and salt and simmer for 5 to 10 minutes.
7. Garnish with the chopped coriander and serve hot.

Nutritive values per serving :

AMT	ENERGY	PROTEIN	CHO	FAT	VIT A	VIT C	CALCIUM	IRON	F.ACID	FIBRE
gm	kcal	gm	gm	gm	mcg	mg	mg	mg	mcg	gm
108	195	10.7	28.4	4.3	306.6	22.3	53.9	2.3	45.1	1.3

Gavarfali ki Subzi

Gavarfali (cluster beans) are rich in iron, folic acid, calcium and are an excellent source of fibre. All these are very important nutrients and are present in good quantities in this humble vegetable.

This Rajasthani recipe is very healthy and delicious too! The addition of curds enhances the calcium as well as the protein levels of the recipe.

Prep. time : 10 min.   Cooking time : 15 min.   Serves 3.

1 cup cluster beans (gavarfali)
½ teaspoon cumin seeds (jeera)
½ teaspoon mustard seeds (rai)
a pinch asafoetida (hing)
½ teaspoon fennel seeds (saunf)
5 curry leaves
1 tablespoon oil
salt to taste

For the curd mixture
½ cup curds (yoghurt)
2 teaspoons coriander (dhania) powder

2 teaspoons chilli powder
¼ teaspoon Bengal gram flour (besan)
salt to taste

1. String the gavarfali by removing the ends and edge
   fibre.
2. Pressure cook the gavarfali in 1 cup of water for 2
   whistles. Keep aside.
3. Combine the curds, coriander powder, chilli powder,
   gram flour and salt and whisk well.
4. Heat the oil in a pan and add the cumin seeds,
   mustard seeds, asafoetida and fennel seeds.
5. Add the curd mixture, curry leaves, 2 tablespoons of
   water and salt and stir continuously.
6. Let the mixture simmer for 5 minutes.
7. Add the gavarfali along with the water used to
   pressure cook it and mix well.
8. Simmer the subzi for a few minutes more.
   Serve hot with rotis.

Nutritive values per serving :

AMT	ENERGY	PROTEIN	CHO	FAT	VIT A	VIT C	CALCIUM	IRON	F.ACID	FIBRE
gm	kcal	gm	gm	gm	mcg	mg	mg	mg	mcg	gm
72	88	1.7	2.4	7.2	114.2	3.1	76.0	0.2	7.7	0.2

Spicy Pineapple Curry

This is a different way of adding fruits to your diet. Ripe diced pineapple is cooked with an aromatic blend of spices and simmered in coconut milk. The iron and the fibre levels in this curry are good and the coconut adds to the protein and energy content.

If you are not fond of pineapple, add a cup of mixed vegetables like peas, carrots, potatoes to the same gravy, and you can also throw in a few cubes of pineapple, if you like.

Prep. time : 10 min.   Cooking time : 10 min.   Serves 3.

1 cup fresh pineapple, peeled and diced
1 teaspoon Bengal gram flour (besan)
1 cup coconut milk
1 teaspoon turmeric powder (haldi)
a pinch asafoetida (hing)
½ teaspoon garam masala
½ teaspoon oil
salt to taste

To be ground into a paste
3 to 4 red chillies
3 tablespoons grated coconut

For the tempering
½ teaspoon mustard seeds (rai)
5 to 6 curry leaves
a pinch asafoetida (hing)
1 teaspoon oil

1. Heat ½ teaspoon of oil, add the asafoetida and pineapple and sauté for 2 minutes.
2. Add the turmeric powder, garam masala, the ground paste and salt and mix well.
3. Add the besan dissolved in 1 cup of water and simmer till the pineapple pieces are tender.

4. For the tempering, heat the oil and add the mustard seeds. When they crackle, add the curry leaves and asafoetida and pour over the curry.
5. Mix well, bring it to a boil and serve hot.

Nutritive values per serving :

AMT	ENERGY	PROTEIN	CHO	FAT	VIT A	VIT C	CALCIUM	IRON	F.ACID	FIBRE
gm	kcal	gm	gm	gm	mcg	mg	mg	mg	mcg	gm
126	343	2.8	14.7	30.3	35.3	23.4	21.1	2.5	2.9	0.7

Healthy Green Curry

The abundance of intensely flavoured ingredients makes this recipe really tasty without the addition of too much fat.

The vegetables are excellent sources of iron, fibre and vitamin C. Quick cooking oats are used to thicken this curry so as to avoid the addition of thickeners like refined flour and cornstarch.

This curry makes a great meal while you're lactating because of the addition of fresh garlic which helps to enhance the production of breast milk.

Prep. time : 15 min.   Cooking time : 20 min.   Serves 4.

½ cup cauliflower florets
½ cup baby corn, cut into roundels
½ cup carrots, diced
½ cup mushrooms, quartered
1 cup spring onions (including greens), chopped
¼ cup quick cooking rolled oats
2 tablespoons butter
salt to taste

To be ground into a paste
1 cup chopped coriander
12 mm. (½") piece ginger, chopped
3 to 4 green chillies
¼ cup fresh green garlic, chopped
juice of ½ lemon

1. Heat the butter in a pan, add the spring onion whites and sauté for 2 to 3 minutes.
2. Add all the vegetables and sauté for 2 to 3 minutes.
3. Add 2 cups of water and salt and bring to a boil.
4. Add the oats and cook for 5 to 7 minutes over a high flame till the vegetables are cooked.
5. Add the ground paste and spring onion greens and allow to boil for 1 minute.
   Serve hot with steamed rice.

Nutritive values per serving :

AMT	ENERGY	PROTEIN	CHO	FAT	VIT A	VIT C	CALCIUM	IRON	F.ACID	FIBRE
gm	kcal	gm	gm	gm	mcg	mg	mg	mg	mcg	gm
73	96	2.2	10.4	5.1	748.1	17.9	33.2	0.8	5.3	0.8

Rotis

Paushtic Roti

The word "paushtic" in Hindi means healthy or life giving. This roti is a nutritious combination of a cereal and a pulse along with a green leafy vegetable, enhanced further by the addition of milk or curds. All of these contribute to make this dish rich in folic acid, iron, protein and calcium.

Have these rotis instead of the plain whole wheat chapatis we usually eat.

Prep. time : 15 min. Cooking time : 20 min. Makes 13 rotis.

1½ cups whole wheat flour (gehun ka atta)
⅓ cup Bengal gram flour (besan)
1 boiled potato, grated
¾ cup chopped spinach (palak)
2 green chillies, chopped
4 tablespoons curds (yoghurt) or milk
1 tablespoon oil
salt ot taste

Other ingredients
2 tablespoons oil for cooking

1. Mix all the ingredients and knead into a dough. Divide into 13 equal portions.
2. Roll out the dough into small rotis with the help of a little flour.
3. Cook on a non-stick tava (griddle) using a little oil. Serve hot.

Nutritive values per roti :

AMT	ENERGY	PROTEIN	CHO	FAT	VIT A	VIT C	CALCIUM	IRON	F.ACID	FIBRE
gm	kcal	gm	gm	gm	mcg	mg	mg	mg	mcg	gm
32	93	2.3	11.4	4.1	265.0	2.1	20.2	0.8	13.0	0.3

Jowar Bajre ki Roti

Picture on cover page

Jowar and bajra flour rotis flavoured with spring onions and green chilli. Jowar and bajra are rich in iron, protein and fibre. Being comparatively dry, this roti is recommended for your first trimester as a it will relieve you of nausea. Have it as a mid morning snack or for lunch with the Usli (page 110).

Prep. time : 5 min. Cooking time : 20 min. Makes 4 rotis.

½ cup bajra flour (black millet flour)
½ cup jowar flour (white millet flour)
1 spring onion, finely chopped
1 green chilli, finely chopped
1 tablespoon oil
salt to taste

1. Combine all the ingredients in a bowl and knead into a soft dough, using warm water as required.
2. Cover and keep aside for 10 minutes.
3. Divide the dough into 4 equal portions.
4. Pat each portion on a dry surface using your palms till it is a circle of 125 mm. (5") diameter.
5. Cook on a tava (griddle) till both sides are lightly browned. Repeat for the remaining circles.
   Serve hot with a vegetable of your choice.

Handy tip

If you want to roll out these rotis instead of patting them, you can do so between 2 sheets of plastic. It is much easier that way.

Nutritive values per roti :

AMT	ENERGY	PROTEIN	CHO	FAT	VIT A	VIT C	CALCIUM	IRON	F.ACID	FIBRE
gm	kcal	gm	gm	gm	mcg	mg	mg	mg	mcg	gm
37	124	2.8	18.0	4.6	55.3	1.0	12.4	1.5	8.5	0.4

Stuffed Bajra Roti

Bajra is the staple diet in many parts of North-Western India where the locals enjoy it with garlic chutney, jaggery and home-made butter.

In this recipe, I have stuffed these rotis with a mixture of paneer, fenugreek and tomatoes, thus enriching it with calcium, folic acid and iron.

If you find it difficult to actually "stuff" these rotis because the dough is a little tough to roll, feel free to knead all the filling ingredients into the dough and then roll out the rotis. It is a much easier way of making them. I also find it easier to roll out this dough between 2 sheets of plastic.

Prep. time : 10 min. Cooking time : 30 min. Makes 8 rotis.

For the dough
1½ cups bajra flour (black millet flour)
pinch salt

To be mixed into a stuffing
½ cup crumbled paneer (cottage cheese)
2 tablespoons chopped fenugreek (methi) leaves
1 green chilli, finely chopped
1 large tomato, finely chopped
salt to taste

Other ingredients
2 tablespoons butter for cooking

1. Combine the bajra flour, salt and enough hot water to make a soft dough.
2. Knead well, divide into 16 portions and roll out each portion into thin rotis.
3. Spread a little stuffing on one roti. Then put another roti on top and press well so that it becomes one roti.
4. Repeat for the remaining rotis and stuffing.
5. Cook each stuffed roti on a tava (griddle) on both sides using a little butter till both sides are golden brown.
   Serve hot.

Nutritive values per roti :

AMT	ENERGY	PROTEIN	CHO	FAT	VIT A	VIT C	CALCIUM	IRON	F.ACID	FIBRE
gm	kcal	gm	gm	gm	mcg	mg	mg	mg	mcg	gm
41	115	3.5	1 3.3	5.3	198.3	3.3	60.8	1.5	11.1	0.3

Paneer Palak Methi Roti

Your nutrient requirement increases during the third trimester, but your appetite may not. So you need to have energy rich foods that are a good combination of 2 to 3 food groups to supplement your needs.

This roti has leafy vegetable and a dairy product which will provide you with calcium, iron and protein in one dish. Have these with a glass of buttermilk or fruit juice to keep you going.

Prep. time : 10 min.   Cooking time : 15 min.   Makes 6 rotis.

For the dough
¾ cup whole wheat flour (gehun ka atta)
1 teaspoon oil
⅓ cup finely chopped fenugreek (methi) leaves and spinach (palak)
1 tablespoon fresh curds (yoghurt)
½ teaspoon chilli powder
¼ teaspoon turmeric powder (haldi)
a pinch asafoetida (hing)
½ teaspoon sugar
salt to taste

For the topping
⅓ cup finely chopped fenugreek (methi) leaves or spinach (palak)
1 tablespoon grated paneer (cottage cheese)

For the dough
1. Combine all the ingredients and knead into a dough. Add more curds if required to make the dough.
2. Divide into 6 portions and roll out into rotis.
3. Cook each roti on a tava till both sides are lightly browned.

How to proceed
When you want to serve, sprinkle a little topping on top of each roti. Place below the grill for 1 minute.
Serve hot.

Nutritive values per roti :

AMT	ENERGY	PROTEIN	CHO	FAT	VIT A	VIT C	CALCIUM	IRON	F.ACID	FIBRE
gm	kcal	gm	gm	gm	mcg	mg	mg	mg	mcg	gm
25	64	2.1	10.2	1.6	282.4	2.1	27.5	0.7	9.8	0.3

Rice Bhakhri

A Maharashtrian friend of mine shared the basic recipe of these bhakris with me. While I was making them at home one day, I tried adding some grated carrots, mint and coriander to add colour to these bhakris. Not only did it add colour to the rotis but the freshness of the mint and coriander complemented the rice flour really well.

These bhakris are packed with carbohydrates, protein and iron. You will relish these with even the simplest of vegetables or a dal.

Prep. time : 20 min.   Cooking time : 20 min.   Makes 6 bhakhris.

For the dough
1 ½ cups whole wheat flour (gehun ka atta)
1 teaspoon oil

For the filling

1 cup rice flour
1 teaspoon oil
½ cup grated carrot
1 green chilli, chopped
2 tablespoons chopped coriander
1 tablespoon mint, chopped
salt to taste

Other ingredients

1 tablespoon oil for cooking

For the dough

1. Combine the flour and oil and knead into a firm dough using enough water.
2. Divide into 6 equal parts and keep aside.

For the filling

1. In a pan, put 1 cup of water to boil with the oil and salt.
2. When it comes to a boil, add the rice flour and mix well using a spoon so that no lumps remain. Cook till the mixture leaves the sides of the pan.
3. Remove from the fire and allow it to cool a little. Knead this dough while it is still warm till it is smooth (for approximately 10 to 12 minutes).
4. Add the carrot, chilli, coriander and mint and mix well.
5. Divide into 6 equal portions and keep aside.

How to proceed

1. Roll out one portion of the dough into a 75 mm. (3") diameter circle.
2. Place a portion of the filling mixture and fold the edges of the dough over the filling.
3. Pinch the edges together to seal the filling in.
4. Flatten the dough and roll again into a 150 mm. (6") diameter circle.
5. Cook on both sides on a tava (griddle) over a medium flame till golden brown in colour, using a little oil.

6. Repeat for the remaining dough and filling to make 5 more bhakhris. Serve hot.

Nutritive values per bhakhri:

AMT	ENERGY	PROTEIN	CHO	FAT	VIT A	VIT C	CALCIUM	IRON	F.ACID	FIBRE
gm	kcal	gm	gm	gm	mcg	mg	mg	mg	mcg	gm
60	203	4.8	35.3	4.8	263.9	1.8	24.0	1.7	13.1	0.7

Garlic Roti

Most people are apprehensive to use garlic as a predominant flavour in their cooking. This aromatic herb is not only good for reducing cholesterol but it actually aids in digestion and also stimulates the production of breast milk.
Unfortunately fresh green garlic is available for only a few months in the year. So if you are making these rotis in the summer, use 4 to 6 large cloves of grated garlic instead of the green garlic and add some fresh coriander leaves to add some colour to the rotis.

Prep. time : 10 min.   Cooking time : 30 min.   Makes 8 rotis.

½ cup jowar flour (white millet flour)
½ cup bajra flour (black millet flour)
½ cup whole wheat flour (gehun ka atta)
½ cup fresh green garlic, chopped
salt to taste

1. **Broccoli Aloo aur Paneer ki Subzi,** *page 107*
2. **Cucumber Curd Rice,** *page 132*

Other ingredients
2 tablespoons oil for cooking

1. Combine all the ingredients in a bowl and knead into a dough adding warm water as required. This dough will not be very pliable and you will not be able to knead it very much.
2. Divide the dough into 8 equal portions and roll out each portion into circles approx. 100 mm. to 125 mm. (4" to 5") in diameter.
3. Cook each roti on a tava (griddle) using a little oil till both sides are golden brown.
   Serve hot.

Nutritive values per roti :

AMT	ENERGY	PROTEIN	CHO	FAT	VIT A	VIT C	CALCIUM	IRON	F.ACID	FIBRE
gm	kcal	gm	gm	gm	mcg	mg	mg	mg	mcg	gm
23	100	2.1	13.2	4.3	46.5	0.0	7.3	1.1	6.4	0.3

1. Spinach Malfatti, *page 138*

Rice

Bajra Khichdi

This is a traditional Rajasthani recipe that we discovered is an excellent source of protein, iron, folic acid and fibre.
Its creamy consistency and mild flavours make it a good recipe to have especially in the preconception period and first trimester. But I'm sure you will enjoy it all through your pregnancy. You can even perk up this khichdi by adding some spices to it and maybe even throw in some vegetables. Serve it with curds or a raita and you have a completely balanced meal ready.

Prep. time : 10 min.   Cooking time : 15 min.   Serves 4.

⅓ cup bajra (black millet), washed
3 tablespoons yellow moong dal (split yellow gram)
1 teaspoon cumin seeds (jeera)
½ teaspoon asafoetida (hing)
2 tablespoons ghee
salt to taste

1. Grind the bajra to a coarse powder in a blender. Keep aside.
2. Wash the ground bajra and moong dal together.
3. Combine the bajra and moong dal with salt and 2½ cups of water and pressure cook for 3 to 4 whistles.
4. Heat the ghee in a pan and add the cumin seeds and asafoetida. When the seeds crackle, pour over the cooked bajra khichdi and mix well.
   Serve hot with kadhi or curds.

Nutritive values per serving :

AMT	ENERGY	PROTEIN	CHO	FAT	VIT A	VIT C	CALCIUM	IRON	F.ACID	FIBRE
gm	kcal	gm	gm	gm	mcg	mg	mg	mg	mcg	gm
32	153	4.1	15.4	8.3	90.5	0.0	13.5	1.5	20.8	0.2

Cabbage Rice

This dish is one that I make when I have no inclination to cook and have some left-over rice. It is really quick to make and tastes good. And since it has no sharp flavours, it will agree with you through your first trimester if you have to deal with morning sickness.

This dish provides appreciable amounts of carbohydrates, protein, calcium and vitamin C.

Prep. time : 10 min.   Cooking time : 20 min.   Serves 4.

1½ cups cooked rice
1 onion, grated
½ cup shredded cabbage
1 capsicum, sliced
½ teaspoon pepper powder
2 tablespoons butter
salt to taste
2 tablespoons grated cheese

1. Heat the butter and sauté the onion for 2 to 3 minutes.
2. Add the cabbage and capsicum and cook for 2 to 3 minutes.
3. Add the rice, pepper and salt and mix well.
4. Sprinkle the cheese on top and serve hot.

Handy tip

Approximately ¾ cup of uncooked rice will yield 1½ cups of cooked rice.

Nutritive values per serving :

AMT	ENERGY	PROTEIN	CHO	FAT	VIT A	VIT C	CALCIUM	IRON	F.ACID	FIBRE
gm	kcal	gm	gm	gm	mcg	mg	mg	mg	mcg	gm
94	146	3.3	20.0	5.8	345.8	61.5	54.2	0.6	5.1	0.6

Cucumber Curd Rice

Picture on page 127

This is a slightly modified version of the South Indian "Dahi Bhaat".

Rich in protein and calcium, this rice dish is just perfect for a cooling summer lunch. The cucumber, carrots and coriander provide fibre and vitamin A. I have used mild flavours, so that it will agree with you even during the first trimester.

Prep. time : 10 min.   Cooking time : 15 min.   Serves 4.

1 cup cooked rice, cooled
1 cup fresh curds (yoghurt)
½ cup cucumber, washed and chopped (unpeeled)
1 cup carrots, grated
¼ cup chopped coriander
salt to taste

For the tempering
1 teaspoon cumin seeds (jeera)
1 to 2 green chillies, slit
1 tablespoon urad dal (split black lentils)
½ teaspoon asafoetida (hing)
4 to 6 curry leaves
1 tablespoon oil

For the garnish
dill leaves (optional)

1. In a large bowl, combine the rice, curds, cucumber, carrots, coriander and salt and mix well.
2. In another pan, heat the oil and add the cumin seeds.
3. When they crackle, add the urad dal, green chillies, asafoetida, curry leaves and sauté for 1 minute.
4. Pour the tempering over the rice and mix well.
   Serve chilled, garnished with dill leaves if you like.

Handy tip

Approximately ½ cup of uncooked rice will yield 1 cup of cooked rice.

Nutritive values per serving :

AMT	ENERGY	PROTEIN	CHO	FAT	VIT A	VIT C	CALCIUM	IRON	F.ACID	FIBRE
gm	kcal	gm	gm	gm	mcg	mg	mg	mg	mcg	gm
111	159	3.7	17.1	7.2	633.7	4.5	130.2	0.6	11.3	0.4

Fada ni Khichdi

A nutritious khichdi made with bulgur wheat, yellow moong dal, vegetables and spices.
You will relish this concoction from the second trimester onwards as your appetite will slowly begin to increase and you will also crave to eat tasty food, unlike the first trimester where only mildly flavoured dishes interested you.
Bulgur wheat in combination with moong dal and vegetables make this dish rich in carbohydrates, vitamin C, iron and fibre.

Prep. time : 15 min.   Cooking time : 40 min.   Serves 4.

1 cup split yellow gram (yellow moong dal)
¾ cup bulgur wheat (dalia)
1 cup potatoes, diced
1 cup green peas
1 cup cauliflower florets
1 cup onions, diced
1 tablespoon ginger- green chilli paste
½ teaspoon whole peppercorns
½ teaspoon turmeric powder (haldi)
1 teaspoon chilli powder
salt to taste

For the tempering
1 stick cinnamon
3 cloves
1 teaspoon cumin seeds (jeera)
½ teaspoon asafoetida (hing)
1 tablespoon ghee

1. Wash and soak the moong dal and bulgur wheat for at least 15 minutes. Drain and keep aside.
2. Bring 4 cups of water to a boil and keep aside.
3. Prepare the tempering by heating the ghee in a pressure cooker, adding the cinnamon, cloves, cumin seeds and asafoetida and stirring for 30 seconds.
4. Add the dal and bulgur wheat together with all the other ingredients and stir for 4 to 5 minutes.
5. Add the hot water and pressure cook for 3 to 4 whistles.
6. Allow the steam to escape and open the pressure cooker.
7. Stir the khichdi vigorously, adding a little hot water if required so that the dal and the bulgur wheat mix well. Serve hot with raita or curds.

Nutritive values per serving:

AMT	ENERGY	PROTEIN	CHO	FAT	VIT A	VIT C	CALCIUM	IRON	F.ACID	FIBRE
gm	kcal	gm	gm	gm	mcg	mg	mg	mg	mcg	gm
179	337	15.4	59.4	4.3	88.0	21.1	69.6	3.9	59.9	2.7

Sprout Pulao

This combination of rice and sprouted legumes (matki) improves the protein quality of the recipe which also provides a good amount of iron, folic acid and vitamin C. We have used matki in this recipe but you can use any other sprouted legume or a combination of sprouts if you like.

This is another good dish for the " tiffin box " to take to work. Your family will love it too.

Prep. time : 20 min.   Cooking time : 15 min.   Serves 4.

1 cup cooked long grained rice
1 cup sprouted matki (math), parboiled
2 cloves
¼ teaspoon asafoetida (hing)
1 green chilli, chopped
1 teaspoon grated ginger
½ capsicum, chopped

4 to 6 spring onions, chopped
1/4 teaspoon turmeric powder (haldi)
1 teaspoon chilli powder
1 teaspoon coriander (dhania) powder
1 tablespoon oil
salt to taste

For the garnish
1 tomato, chopped
2 tablespoons chopped coriander

1. Heat the oil, add the cloves and asafoetida and sauté for a few seconds.
2. Add the green chilli, ginger, capsicum and spring onions and sauté for 2 to 3 minutes.
3. Add the turmeric powder, chilli powder, coriander powder and the sprouted matki and mix well.
4. Add 1/4 cup of water and salt and simmer over a slow flame till the matki is cooked.
5. Add the rice and toss well.
   Serve hot, garnished with the chopped tomato and coriander.

Handy tip

To sprout matki, soak them in water for 6 to 8 hours. Then tie them in a damp muslin cloth. They will sprout in about 24 to 36 hours in warm weather.

Nutritive values per serving :

AMT	ENERGY	PROTEIN	CHO	FAT	VIT A	VIT C	CALCIUM	IRON	F.ACID	FIBRE
gm	kcal	gm	gm	gm	mcg	mg	mg	mg	mcg	gm
96	159	5.2	25.3	4.1	107.7	28.7	54.6	1.9	3.9	1.1

Wholesome Khichdi

Khichdi is a meal that is complete in itself. It is a misconception that khichdi is meant only for sick people. I have added grated vegetables to add more fibre to this recipe.

The rice and dal provide plenty of protein and carbohydrates and also folic acid.

This recipe is good throughout your pregnancy, but it is best suited for the third trimester and lactation because it is a concentrated source of nutrients which you will require throughout this period.

Prep. time : 10 min.   Cooking time : 25 min.   Serves 4.

⅔ cup rice
⅔ cup moong dal (split yellow gram)
1 cup grated bottle gourd (doodhi/lauki)
1 cup grated carrot
½ teaspoon turmeric powder (haldi)
1 teaspoon cumin seeds (jeera)
½ teaspoon asafoetida (hing)
6 peppercorns
1 bay leaf
4 cloves
½ tablespoon ghee
salt to taste

1. Wash the rice and moong dal together and keep aside.
2. Heat the ghee and add the cumin seeds. When they crackle, add the asafoetida, peppercorns, bay leaf and cloves.
3. Add the bottle gourd and carrot and sauté for a few seconds.
4. Add the dal, rice, turmeric powder, salt and 3 cups of water and pressure cook for 3 whistles.
5. When done, whisk the khichdi to combine the rice and dal together.
   Serve hot with fresh curds.

Nutritive values per serving :

AMT	ENERGY	PROTEIN	CHO	FAT	VIT A	VIT C	CALCIUM	IRON	F.ACID	FIBRE
gm	kcal	gm	gm	gm	mcg	mg	mg	mg	mcg	gm
95	192	7.5	35.3	2.3	443.8	0.7	42.0	1.4	37.1	0.6

Continental

Spinach Malfatti

Picture on page 128

Try this dish for an early pregnancy boost. Mildly spiced and rich in iron, calcium, folic acid and protein, this is a really delicious recipe which I am sure you will enjoy.

Prep. time : 25 min.   Cooking time : 25 min.
Serves 4.   Baking temperature : 200°C (400°F).
                                      Baking time : 15 min.

For the spinach dumplings
3 cups finely chopped spinach (palak) leaves
¾ cup crumbled paneer (cottage cheese)
2 pinches nutmeg (jaiphal) powder
½ teaspoon chopped green chilli
2 tablespoons plain flour (maida)
2 pinches baking powder
salt to taste

For the tomato sauce
1½ cups tomato pulp
1 tablespoon garlic, chopped
2 spring onions, chopped
1 tablespoon chilli flakes (paprika)
1 teaspoon chilli powder
2 tablespoons tomato purée
4 tablespoons milk
2 tablespoons olive oil or oil
salt to taste

For the topping
¼ cup grated cheese or paneer

For the spinach dumplings
1. Steam the spinach leaves for 5 minutes and squeeze out the water. Keep it aside for use in the tomato sauce.
2. Mix all the ingredients and shape into small balls.
3. Steam for 5 minutes. Keep aside.

138

For the tomato sauce

1. Heat the olive oil, add the garlic and spring onions and sauté for 1 minute.
2. Add the tomato pulp and cook till the sauce thickens.
3. Add the chilli flakes, chilli powder, tomato purée, salt and ½ cup of water and bring to a boil (use the drained spinach liquid instead of water).
4. Add the milk. Mix well and keep aside.

How to proceed

1. Place the dumplings in a greased baking dish.
2. Pour the tomato sauce on top and sprinkle the grated cheese on top.
3. Bake in a pre-heated oven at 200° C (400° F) for 15 minutes.
   Serve hot.

Nutritive values per serving :

AMT	ENERGY	PROTEIN	CHO	FAT	VIT A	VIT C	CALCIUM	IRON	F.ACID	FIBRE
gm	kcal	gm	gm	gm	mcg	mg	mg	mg	mcg	gm
174	278	8.3	13.2	20.8	3219.7	25.8	294.0	1.1	74.2	0.7

Baked Potatoes with Broccoli and Red Pepper

Potatoes are an excellent food choice in your first trimester and even the pre-pregnancy period when you need to stock up on folic acid and iron. The skin of the potato (which we always discard) is edible and is a rich source of folic acid. If you scrub the potatoes really well before you cook them, you do not really need to peel them. Broccoli is another good source of folic acid apart from providing for plenty of fibre. The cheese and cream add calcium to this dish and the red pepper is great for vitamin C.

Prep. time : 5 min.   Baking time : 10 min.
Makes 6 potatoes.   Baking temperature : 160°C (320°F)

6 large potatoes, boiled and unpeeled
salt to taste

For the filling

1 cup broccoli, finely chopped
1 cup red pepper (capsicum), finely chopped
3 cloves garlic, finely chopped
3 cloves garlic, finely chopped
2 to 3 green chillies, finely chopped
4 tablespoons cream
1½ cups mozzarella cheese or cooking cheese, grated
2 tablespoons butter
salt and pepper to taste

For the filling

1. Heat the butter in a pan, add the broccoli, red pepper, garlic and green chillies and sauté for 2 to 3 minutes.
2. Add the cream, salt and pepper and sauté for 2 more minutes. Remove from the fire.
3. Add the cheese and mix well.

How to proceed

1. Cut each boiled potato into 2 halves horizontally.
2. Scoop the potato halves, using a spoon so that a depression is created for the filling.
3. Sprinkle each potato half with some salt. Fill the potato halves with the filling mixture and mound it up slightly.
4. Bake in a pre-heated oven at 200°C (400°F) for 10 minutes or until the cheese melts.
   Serve hot.

Handy tip

If the potatoes have been refrigerated after they have been boiled, then you will have to bake them in the oven for at least 10 to 12 minutes at a lower temperature approx.160°C (320°F) before you fill them.

Nutritive values per potato :

AMT	ENERGY	PROTEIN	CHO	FAT	VIT A	VIT C	CALCIUM	IRON	F.ACID	FIBRE
gm	kcal	gm	gm	gm	mcg	mg	mg	mg	mcg	gm
111	195	6.4	17.5	11.1	465.8	19.6	179.4	0.8	10.0	0.4

Broccoli and Baby Corn Stir Fry

Tired of dal-chawal? Then this is just the thing you need. A simple stir fry with oriental origins that is rich in fibre, folic acid, protein and above all taste. Toss in some noodles if you want to make a bigger meal of this dish.

Prep. time : 10 min.   Cooking time : 5 min.   Serves 4.

¾ cup broccoli or cauliflower (blanched), cut into big pieces
⅓ cup baby corn, sliced diagonally
⅓ cup capsicums, cut into big pieces
⅓ cup onions, cut into big pieces
2 tablespoons french beans (parboiled)
a few pieces cucumber, diagonally sliced
7 to 8 cashewnuts, lightly toasted
1 teaspoon finely chopped garlic
1 tablespoon cornflour
a pinch sugar
2 pinches black pepper powder
2 tablespoons oil
salt to taste

1. Heat the oil in a wok or frying pan on a high flame. Add the garlic and stir fry over a high flame for a few seconds.
2. Add the capsicums, onions, broccoli, baby corn, french beans and cucumber and stir fry for 2 minutes.
3. Mix the cornflour with ½ cup of water and add to the mixture.
4. Add the black pepper, sugar and salt and cook for 1 minute.
   Serve hot topped with the toasted cashewnuts.

Nutritive values per serving :

AMT	ENERGY	PROTEIN	CHO	FAT	VIT A	VIT C	CALCIUM	IRON	F.ACID	FIBRE
gm	kcal	gm	gm	gm	mcg	mg	mg	mg	mcg	gm
60	107	1.6	6.0	8.6	366.3	25.9	20.9	0.5	9.1	0.5

Easy Cheesy Vegetable Pasta

This pasta dish is satisfying because of its high carbohydrate content which is beneficial for you especially during your first trimester and also while you are lactating. The milk and cheese are good sources of protein and calcium while the other ingredients supplement this recipe with iron, folic acid, fibre and vitamin C.

Picture on page 102

Prep. time : 10 min.   Cooking time : 10 min.   Serves 4.

2 cups cooked pasta (penne, macaroni or fusilli)
1 onion, sliced
1 tablespoon celery, chopped
½ cup capsicum, sliced
1 cup boiled vegetables (carrots, peas, french beans, broccoli, red pepper etc.), diced
¾ cup milk
3 cheese slices (or ½ cup grated cheese)
½ teaspoon dried mixed herbs
1 teaspoon butter
salt and pepper to taste

1. Heat the butter in a pan and sauté the onion, celery and capsicum for 2 minutes.
2. Add the milk and cheese slices and bring to a boil.
3. Add the vegetables, mixed herbs, salt and pepper and mix well.
4. Toss the cooked pasta in the sauce and bring to a boil. Serve hot with toast or garlic bread.

Handy tip

Approximately 1¼ cups of dried pasta will yield 2 cups of cooked pasta.

Nutritive values per serving :

AMT	ENERGY	PROTEIN	CHO	FAT	VIT A	VIT C	CALCIUM	IRON	F.ACID	FIBRE
gm	kcal	gm	gm	gm	mcg	mg	mg	mg	mcg	gm
159	269	11.4	36.4	7.5	551.0	33.1	239.6	2.5	19.3	0.9

Vegetable Stew

This nourishing aromatic broth is good for those days when you feel least inclined to cook up a whole meal. Try this when your appetite is better in second and third trimesters.

This make a great one dish meal when served with hot dinner rolls or steamed rice. Packed with fibre, protein and iron, this dish is one your family will also love.

Prep. time : 15 min.   Cooking time : 20 min.   Serves 4.

1 onion, sliced
4 to 6 peppercorns
1 clove
1 stick cinnamon
1½ teaspoons garlic, chopped
1 tablespoon celery, chopped
1 cup sliced mushrooms
1 cup carrots, cut into thin strips
1 cup capsicum, cut into thin strips
1 tablespoon plain flour (maida)
1 tablespoon fresh cream
1 tablespoon butter
salt to taste

1. Heat the butter and sauté the onion slices till they are lightly browned.
2. Add the peppercorns, clove and cinnamon.
3. Add the garlic, celery, mushrooms, carrots and capsicum and sauté till they are lightly browned in colour and all the liquid has evaporated.

4. Add the flour and cook for another 4 to 5 minutes till the flour is light brown in colour.
5. Add 1½ cups of water and bring to a boil, stirring continuously so that no lumps remain.
6. Allow to simmer for 5 to 7 minutes adding a little more water if required.
7. Add the fresh cream and serve hot with bread rolls or plain rice.

Nutritive values per serving :

AMT	ENERGY	PROTEIN	CHO	FAT	VIT A	VIT C	CALCIUM	IRON	F.ACID	FIBRE
gm	kcal	gm	gm	gm	mcg	mg	mg	mg	mcg	gm
111	72	1.5	8.7	3.6	852.2	45.8	48.2	1.0	10.0	1.1

Desserts

Carrot Pancakes

If you have an insatiable sweet tooth, try desserts like this one that is healthier and will leave you satisfied. These yummy carrot halwa stuffed pancakes are delightful.

I have experimented with an easier and healthier version of Gajar ka Halwa. You don't have to slave for hours to make a rich calorie laden halwa. The carrots are first steamed and then sautéed in a little ghee. I have also used skimmed milk powder instead of whole milk. The milk powder gives it a rich milky flavour of khoya and also cuts out all the extra calories which whole milk would have added.

A great dish for entertaining too!

Prep. time : 20 min.

Cooking time : 40 min.
Makes 12 pancakes.

For the pancakes
½ cup plain flour (maida)
½ cup cornflour
¾ cup milk
a pinch salt
2 teaspoons melted butter

For the carrot halwa
3 cups grated carrots
4 tablespoons sugar
5 tablespoons skimmed milk powder
2 teaspoons almonds, sliced
a pinch cardamom (elaichi) powder
2 tablespoons ghee

For the pancakes
1. Mix the plain flour, cornflour, milk, salt and ½ cup of water. Mix well ensuring that no lumps remain.
2. Grease a 125 mm. (5") diameter non-stick pan with a little butter.

145

3. Pour 2 tablespoons of the batter and tilt the pan around quickly so that the batter coats the pan evenly.
4. When the sides start to peel off, turn the pancake around and cook the other side for 30 seconds.
5. Repeat for the remaining batter, greasing the pan with butter when required and make 11 more pancakes.

For the carrot halwa
1. Steam the grated carrots over boiling water for 3 minutes.
2. Heat the ghee, add the steamed carrots and sauté for 2 minutes.
3. Add the sugar and cook for 2 to 3 minutes. Then add the milk powder and cook for a few minutes, stirring continuously.
4. Add the almonds and sprinkle the cardamom powder on top.
6. Mix well and keep aside. Divide into 12 portions.

How to proceed
Spread a portion of the halwa on each pancake and roll up. Serve immediately.

Nutritive values per pancake :

AMT	ENERGY	PROTEIN	CHO	FAT	VIT A	VIT C	CALCIUM	IRON	F.ACID	FIBRE
gm	kcal	gm	gm	gm	mcg	mg	mg	mg	mcg	gm
55	113	2.3	13.8	5.1	519.4	1.1	74.0	0.5	4.0	0.3

Pineapple Crumble

Picture on page 102

Slow baked pineapples are a sweet and nourishing dessert or snack. Rich in potassium, iron and fibre, this dish is just perfect to enjoy with a cup of hot chocolate as a midnight snack. Topped with a crispy cinnamon and oatmeal crumble, this is a healthier version of the traditional butter rich and refined flour crumble we usually make.
You can also try making this crumble with fresh peaches or apples, instead of the pineapple.

Prep. time : 15 min.   Baking time : 25 min.
Serves 4.   Baking temperature : 180°C (360°F).

1½ cups chopped fresh pineapple
¾ cup brown sugar
½ cup whole wheat flour (gehun ka atta)
½ cup quick cooking rolled oats
¾ teaspoon cinnamon (dalchini) powder
¾ teaspoon nutmeg (jaiphal) powder
2 tablespoons butter
¼ cup chopped almonds, cashew and walnuts
butter to grease

1. Combine the pineapple with ½ cup of brown sugar and place in a greased ovenproof bowl, approximately 150 mm. (6") in diameter.
2. In another bowl, combine the flour, oats, cinnamon powder, nutmeg powder, butter and the remaining sugar and mix well using your fingertips, till the mixture resembles bread crumbs.
3. Sprinkle the mixture on top of the pineapple and top up with the chopped nuts.
4. Bake in a pre-heated oven at 180°C (360°F) for 25 minutes or till the topping is golden brown.
5. Serve hot with a scoop of ice-cream if you like.

Handy tip

If the pineapple is not completely ripe, sauté it in little butter till all the liquid evaporates and then add the sugar. Follow the recipe from step 2 onwards.

Nutritive values per serving :

AMT	ENERGY	PROTEIN	CHO	FAT	VIT A	VIT C	CALCIUM	IRON	F.ACID	FIBRE
gm	kcal	gm	gm	gm	mcg	mg	mg	mg	mcg	gm
119	303	4.6	49.1	9.7	192.8	24.3	33.1	2.9	8.0	1.0

Lapsi

A sumptuous dessert, made from broken wheat, that is light enough to be eaten after a heavy meal when you still crave for sugar. It will nourish you with energy, protein and iron.

Prep. time : 5 min. Cooking time : 20 min. Serves 4.

½ cup bulgur wheat (dalia)
½ cup sugar
½ teaspoon cardamom (elaichi) powder
2 tablespoons sliced almonds
3 tablespoons warm milk
3 tablespoons pure ghee

1. Heat the ghee in a pan and fry the broken wheat, stirring continuously till it is golden brown in colour.
2. Meanwhile, heat 1½ cups of water in another pan till warm.
3. Add the water to the bulgur wheat and increase the flame till the water comes to a boil.
4. Then reduce the flame and cook, stirring occasionally till the wheat is almost done.
5. Add the sugar, cardamom powder and almonds and mix well.
6. Cook on a slow flame till the ghee separates.
7. Allow the lapsi to cool for some time.
8. Before serving, add the milk and heat again.
   Serve hot.

Handy tip

If the lapsi becomes dry while cooking, add some water or milk.

Nutritive values per serving :

AMT	ENERGY	PROTEIN	CHO	FAT	VIT A	VIT C	CALCIUM	IRON	F.ACID	FIBRE
gm	kcal	gm	gm	gm	mcg	mg	mg	mg	mcg	gm
65	263	2.2	38.6	10.7	105.2	0.1	32.4	1.0	0.6	0.6

Eggless Caramel Custard

This custard is a good alternative for those who hate drinking plain milk. It is a light and tasty pudding with a good amount of calcium, energy and protein.

Prep. time : 1 hour.   Cooking time : 10 min.   Serves 6.

2½ cups milk
3 teaspoons custard powder
¼ cup sugar
½ teaspoon vanilla essence
10 teaspoons (5 grams) china grass , cut into small pieces
2 tablespoons sugar for caramelising

1. Soak the china grass in ¾ cup of cold water for 1 hour. Simmer over a slow flame until it dissolves and becomes a clear liquid.
2. In a pudding mould (approx. 6 inches (150 mm) in diameter) add the sugar for caramelising and 1 teaspoon of water and continue cooking until it becomes brown. Spread it all over the mould, rotating the mould to the caramelised sugar evenly. The sugar will harden in 10 minutes.
3. Keep aside ½ cup of milk. Mix the custard powder in this cold milk.
4. Boil the remaining milk with the sugar. When the milk starts boiling, add the custard and continue cooking until you get a smooth sauce.
5. Add the melted china grass to the custard. Boil again for 2 minutes. Strain the mixture and cool it slightly.
6. Add the vanilla essence. Mix well. Pour this mixture over the prepared mould.
7. Refrigerate till it sets.
8. Before serving, loosen the sides with a sharp knife and invert on a plate.

Nutritive values per serving :

AMT	ENERGY	PROTEIN	CHO	FAT	VIT A	VIT C	CALCIUM	IRON	F.ACID	FIBRE
gm	kcal	gm	gm	gm	mcg	mg	mg	mg	mcg	gm
83	119	3.2	11.5	4.9	120.0	0.8	157.5	0.2	4.2	0.0

Kalakand

If made in the traditional way, kalakand is a very time consuming and intricate mithai to make.

I found a much easier way to make kalakand in a few minutes and believe me, it tastes just as good.

Packed with calcium and protein, this energy rich recipe is just what you need to perk you up on a slow day.

As always with desserts, remember that moderation is the keyword here.

Prep. time : 10 min.   Cooking time : 15 min.   Makes 16 pieces.

¾ cup unsalted fresh paneer (cottage cheese)
8 tablespoons whole milk powder
¼ cup sugar
½ cup cream
½ teaspoon cardamom (elaichi) powder

For the garnish
10 almonds, slivered

1. Combine all the ingredients in a non-stick pan.
2. Cook over a medium flame, stirring continuously for approximately 10 to 15 minutes till the mixture thickens and leaves the sides of the pan.
3. Spread onto a 175 mm. (7") diameter pie dish. Cool and cut into 16 pieces.
4. Garnish with the slivered almonds and serve chilled.

Handy tip

Use fresh paneer for best results.

Nutritive values per piece :

AMT	ENERGY	PROTEIN	CHO	FAT	VIT A	VIT C	CALCIUM	IRON	F.ACID	FIBRE
gm	kcal	gm	gm	gm	mcg	mg	mg	mg	mcg	gm
20	71	2.1	5.1	4.7	111.6	0.4	71.5	0.1	0.2	0.0

Badam ka Sheera

Milk and almonds prove to be a good combination during your lactation period. These foods help to stimulate the production of breast milk. The calcium and the energy content of the recipe are good due to the addition of milk into the sheera.
Have a tablespoon every day while you are lactating.

Prep. time : 15 min.   Cooking time : 30 min.   Makes ¾ cup.

½ cup almonds, soaked overnight
⅓ cup milk
4 tablespoons sugar
3 tablespoons ghee
¼ teaspoon cardamom (elaichi) powder

For the garnish
2 to 3 almonds, sliced

1. Pour 1 cup of boiling water over the almonds. Leave aside for 5 minutes.
2. Drain and remove the skins of the almonds.
3. Purée the almonds with 4 tablespoons of milk to a smooth paste in a blender.
4. Heat the ghee in a kadhai and add the almond purée. Cook over a slow flame while stirring continuously till the mixture turns golden brown (approx. 15 minutes).
5. Combine the milk and 4 tablespoons of water and bring to a boil. Add this to the cooked almond mixture and simmer for 2 to 3 minutes.
6. Add the sugar, cardamom powder and cook till the sugar has dissolved while stirring continuously.
7. Serve hot garnished with the sliced almonds.

Nutritive values per tablespoon:

AMT	ENERGY	PROTEIN	CHO	FAT	VIT A	VIT C	CALCIUM	IRON	F.ACID	FIBRE
gm	kcal	gm	gm	gm	mcg	mg	mg	mg	mcg	gm
19	94	1.1	6.0	7.2	47.9	0.1	21.3	0.2	0.3	0.1

Preconception

Although all the recipes can be enjoyed during most of your pregnancy, I have sorted them out keeping in mind your nutritional requirements for each trimester.
During the preconception periods you need to stock on plenty of **folic acid** and **iron** to prepare for a healthy pregnancy.

Recipes	Page No.	Energy	Protein	Calcium	Iron	Folic Acid	Fibre	VIT A	VIT C
Date and Banana Shake	46	✓	✓	✓	✓				
Dal and Vegetable Idli	52	✓	✓		✓	✓		✓	
Soya Upma	53	✓	✓	✓	✓	✓	✓	✓	✓
Lentil and Vegetable Broth	81		✓		✓	✓			
Broccoli Broth	83				✓	✓	✓	✓	
Sweet Corn and Kidney Bean Salad	92	✓	✓	✓			✓		
Energy Salad	93	✓	✓		✓		✓	✓	✓
Hariyali Dal	105	✓	✓	✓	✓	✓		✓	
Soya Mutter ki Subzi	106	✓	✓	✓	✓	✓	✓	✓	
Paushtic Roti	120		✓	✓	✓			✓	
Bajra Khichdi	130	✓	✓		✓	✓			
Spinach Malfatti	138	✓	✓		✓	✓		✓	✓
Carrot Pancakes	145	✓	✓	✓				✓	
Pineapple Crumble	146	✓	✓		✓			✓	✓

✓ *The symbol shows that the recipe is rich in the indicated nutrient.*

First trimester

For the first trimester, apart from **folic acid** and **iron**, you will also need plenty of **calcium** and **protein**. So enjoy these delightful delicacies.

Recipes	Page No.	Energy	Protein	Calcium	Iron	Folic Acid	Fibre	VIT A	VIT C
Fig and Apricot Shake	49	✓	✓	✓	✓			✓	
Moong Dal Dosa	54	✓	✓	✓	✓	✓			
Methi Palak Dhokla	56	✓	✓	✓	✓	✓		✓	
Golpapdi	64	✓	✓		✓				
Whole Wheat Methi Khakhras	65	✓	✓		✓	✓	✓		
Til Chikki	66	✓	✓	✓	✓	✓			
Bajra Khakhras	68	✓	✓				✓		
Healthy Tomato Soup	84		✓	✓	✓	✓		✓	✓
Potato and Carrot Soup	85	✓						✓	
Three Bean Salad	91	✓	✓	✓	✓	✓	✓		✓
Fruity Bean Salad	94	✓	✓	✓	✓	✓	✓	✓	✓
Orange Sesame Tabbouleh	96		✓		✓	✓	✓		✓
Broccoli Aloo aur Paneer ki subzi	107		✓	✓	✓	✓	✓	✓	
Dahi Chane ki Subzi	108	✓	✓	✓				✓	
Jowar Bajre ki Roti	121	✓	✓	✓	✓	✓	✓		
Cabbage Rice	131	✓	✓	✓				✓	✓
Cucumber Curd Rice	132	✓	✓	✓				✓	
Baked Potatoes with Broccoli and Red Pepper	139	✓	✓	✓		✓		✓	
Lapsi	148	✓	✓	✓	✓			✓	

✓ *The symbol shows that the recipe is rich in the indicated nutrient.*

Second trimester

It is important to add more **fibre** to your diet along with the other essential nutrients during the second trimester to combat any disgestive discomforts you may face.

Recipes	Page No.	Energy	Protein	Calcium	Iron	Folic Acid	Fibre	VIT A	VIT C
Pineapple Passion	47	✓		✓	✓		✓	✓	✓
Gauva Drink	48	✓					✓		
Bulgur Wheat Pancakes	59	✓	✓		✓				
Chocolate Chip and Oatmeal Cookies	69	✓	✓		✓			✓	
Sprout and Fruit Bhel	70	✓	✓	✓	✓				✓
High Fibre Bread	71	✓	✓	✓	✓	✓	✓		
High Fibre Bhakri	72	✓	✓	✓	✓	✓	✓		
Spinach and Panner Soup	86	✓	✓	✓	✓	✓		✓	
Golden Broth	87	✓	✓	✓	✓			✓	
Stir Fry Salad	97	✓	✓	✓	✓		✓	✓	
Chick Pea Salad	98	✓	✓	✓	✓	✓	✓	✓	
Usli	110	✓	✓	✓	✓		✓		
Sai Bhaji	111	✓	✓	✓	✓	✓			
Stuffed Bajra Roti	122	✓	✓	✓	✓	✓		✓	
Fada ni Khichdi	133	✓	✓	✓	✓	✓	✓		✓
Broccoli and Baby Corn Stir Fry	141	✓	✓				✓	✓	✓
Eggless Caramel Custard	149	✓	✓	✓				✓	

✓ *The symbol shows that the recipe is rich in the indicated nutrient.*

Third trimester

In this trimester you will need to have **nutrient dense** foods that will satiate you even if you consume small quantities and will provide you with all the required nourishment.

Recipes	Page No.	Energy	Protein	Calcium	Iron	Folic Acid	Fibre	VIT A	VIT C
Honey Banana Shake	49	✓	✓	✓					
Buckwheat Pancake	60	✓	✓	✓	✓		✓		
Thalipeeth	73	✓	✓	✓	✓		✓	✓	
Mooli Muthias	74	✓	✓	✓	✓				
Bean Soup	88		✓	✓		✓		✓	
Tossed Salad	99		✓	✓	✓		✓	✓	✓
Fruit and Lettuce Salad	100	✓	✓	✓	✓		✓		✓
Paatal Bhaji (Colocasia Ambti)	112	✓	✓	✓	✓	✓		✓	
Subzi Dal	114	✓	✓	✓	✓	✓		✓	
Paneer Palak Methi Roti	123	✓	✓	✓	✓		✓	✓	
Rice Bhakhri	124	✓	✓		✓			✓	
Sprout Pulao	134	✓	✓	✓	✓	✓	✓		
Vegetable Stew	143	✓	✓		✓				✓
Kalakand	150	✓	✓	✓				✓	

✓ *The symbol shows that the recipe is rich in the indicated nutrient.*

Lactation

During lactation you need to supplement your diet with plenty of **Calcium**, **Iron**, **vitamin A** and **vitamin C**. Also we have included foods like **garlic**, **methi**, **almonds** which will enhance the production of breast milk.

Recipes	Page No.	Energy	Protein	Calcium	Iron	Folic Acid	Fibre	VIT A	VIT C
My Fair Lady	50	✓	✓	✓					
Strawberry Chickoo Shake	51	✓	✓	✓	✓			✓	✓
Banana Walnut Pancakes	62	✓	✓	✓			✓	✓	
Gaund Golpapdi	65	✓	✓	✓	✓	✓			
Baked Methi Puris	78		✓	✓	✓		✓	✓	
Mukhwas	79	✓	✓	✓	✓				
Winter Vegetable Soup	89	✓	✓	✓	✓				
Cabbage and Moong Dal Salad	104		✓	✓	✓		✓		
Gavarfali ki Subzi	115	✓	✓	✓	✓	✓	✓	✓	
Spicy Pineapple Curry	117	✓	✓		✓		✓		✓
Healthy Green Curry	118	✓	✓		✓			✓	
Garlic Roti	126	✓	✓		✓		✓		
Wholesome Khichdi	136	✓	✓	✓	✓	✓		✓	
Easy Cheesy Vegetable Pasta	142	✓	✓	✓					
Badam ka Sheera	151	✓	✓	✓				✓	

✓ The symbol shows that the recipe is rich in the indicated nutrient.

Folic Acid Rich Foods

The requirement of folic acid during pregnancy is 400 mcg per day. Rich sources of folic acid are cereals, pulses and green leafy vegetables. The following table gives the quantification of these food sources in descending order.

Ingredients	mcg/cup
Kabuli chana, cooked	305
Chana dal (Split Bengal gram), cooked	242
Chawli beans (Cow peas), cooked	233
Yellow moong dal (Split yellow gram), cooked	213
Urad dal (Split black lentils), cooked	199
Soyabean, cooked	175
Toovar dal (Arhar), cooked	169
Til (Sesame seeds)	161
Gavarfali (Cluster beans), chopped	144
Chawli leaves (Cowpea leaves), chopped	101
Palak (Spinach), chopped	84
Bhindi (Ladies finger), chopped	74
Soyabean flour	68
Tomato, chopped	47
Fansi (French beans), chopped	46
Bajra flour (Black millet flour)	44
Gehun ka atta (Whole wheat flour)	39
Peanuts (Groundnuts)	27
Phudina (Mint leaves), chopped	11

All the nutritive values are calculated for 1 standard cup (200 ml.)
Please note that the weight per cup for each food will vary depending on its bulk density.

Iron Rich Foods

The requirement of iron during pregnancy is 38 mg per day. Rich sources of iron are cereals, pulses, green leafy vegetables and nuts. The following table gives the quantification of these food sources in descending order.

Ingredients	mg/cup
Soyabean, cooked	18.2
Chawli beans (Cow peas), cooked	15.6
Matki (Moath beans), soaked and cooked	15.6
Chawli leaves (Cowpea leaves), chopped	15.6
Kurmure (Puffed rice)	12.0
Til (Sesame seeds)	11.1
Cauliflower leaves, chopped	10.4
Masoor dal (split red lentils), cooked	10.0
Kismis (Raisins)	9.2
Moong dal (Split yellow gram), cooked	8.0
Rajma (Kidney beans), soaked and cooked	8.0
Bajra four(Black millet flour)	7.7
Pista (Pistachios)	7.7
Kharek (Dry dates), chopped	7.6
Kabuli chana (Chick peas), cooked	7.5
Chana dal (Split Bengal gram), cooked	7.5
Soyabean flour	7.1
Kaju (Cashewnuts)	5.8
Urad dal (Spilt black lentils)	5.7
Gehun ka atta (Whole wheat flour)	5.3
Ukda chawal (Parboiled rice), cooked	4.5
Ajwain ka patta, chopped	4.5
Arvi ke patte (Colocasia leaves), chopped	4.4
Toovar (Arhar Dal), cooked	4.0
Jowar flour (White millet flour)	4.0
Gur (Jaggery), chopped	4.0
Nachni flour (Ragi flour)	3.9
Kopra (Dry coconut), grated	3.9
Shepu (Dill), chopped	3.5
Peanuts (Groundnuts)	3.4
Pineapple, cubed	3.1
Akhrot (Walnuts)	3.0
Phudina (Mint leaves), chopped	1.6
Poha (Beaten rice)	1.0

All the nutritive values are calculated for 1 standard cup (200 ml.)
Please note that the weight per cup for each food will vary depending on its bulk density.

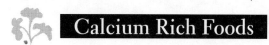

Calcium Rich Foods

The requirement of calcium (Ca) during pregnancy is 1000 mg per day. Rich sources of calcium are milk and milk products, green leafy vegetables and dals. The following table gives the quantification of these food sources in descending order.

Ingredients	mg/cup	Ingredients	mg/cup
Til (Sesame seeds)	1740	Chawli beans (Cow peas), soaked and cooked	135
Whole milk paneer, shredded	730	Gavarfali (Cluster beans), chopped	130
Whole milk paneer, cubes	691	Kharek (Dry dates), chopped	125
Cheese, shredded	632	Gur (Jaggery), chopped	120
Buffalo's milk	420	Arhar (Toovar) dal	120
Buffalo's milk curds (Yoghurt)	420	Moong dal (Split yellow gram), cooked	114
Soyabean, cooked	420	Moong dal flour (Green gram dal flour)	114
Rajma (Kidney beans), soaked and cooked	406	Methi (Fenugreek leaves), chopped	111
Nachni flour (Ragi flour)	344	Akhrot (Walnuts)	106
Kabuli chana (Chick peas), cooked	331	Peanuts (Groundnuts)	105
Chawli leaves (Cowpea), chopped	270	Masoor dal (Split red lentils), cooked	105
Cow's milk	240	Arvi ke patte (Colocasia leaves), chopped	102
Cow's milk curds (Yoghurt)	240	Whole masoor (Red lentils), cooked	92
Skim milk	240	Chana dal (Split Bengal gram), cooked	92
Skim milk curds (Yoghurt)	240	Mooli ke patte (Radish leaves), chopped	80
Urad dal (Split black lentils), cooked	233	Gehun ka atta (Whole wheat flour)	52
Badam (Almonds)	230	Palak (Spinach), chopped	50
Kopra (Dry coconut), grated	200	Fansi (French beans), chopped	46
Skim milk paneer, shredded	182	Besan (Bengal gram flour)	46
Moong (Green gram), sprouted and cooked	180	Dhania (Coriander leaves), chopped	46
Skim milk paneer, cubes	173	Shepu (Dill), chopped	38
Soyabean flour	163		
Cauliflower leaves, chopped	163		
Pista (Pistachios)	140		

All the nutritive values are calculated for 1 standard cup (200 ml.)
Please note that the weight per cup for each food will vary depending on its bulk density.

Fibre Rich Foods

The requirement of fibre during pregnancy is 25 to 30 mg per day. Rich sources of fibre are cereals, pulses, green leafy vegetables and raw fruits. The following table gives the quantification of these food sources in descending order.

Ingredients	mg/cup
Rajma (Kidney beans) soaked and cooked	7.5
Whole moong (Whole green gram), cooked	7.4
Matki (Math beans), soaked and cooked	7.4
Kabuli chana (Chick peas), cooked	6.4
Khajur (Fresh dates), chopped	5.4
Amla	5.0
Peanuts (Groundnuts)	4.2
Kharek (Dry dates), chopped	4.1
Nachni flour (Ragi flour)	3.6
Fresh coconut, grated	3.6
Til (Sesame seeds)	3.5
Kopra (Dry coconut), grated	3.3
Gavarfali (Cluster beans), chopped	3.2
Soyabean, cooked	2.5
Gehun ka atta (Whole wheat flour)	2.1
Green peas	2.1
Pista (Pistachios)	2.1
Akhrot (Walnuts)	2.0
Fansi (French beans), chopped	1.8
Baingan (Brinjal), chopped	1.6
Papadi beans (Broad beans), chopped	1.6
Suran (Yam), chopped	1.3
Simla mirch (Capsicum), chopped	1.2
Seb (Apple), diced	1.2
Gajar (Carrots), shredded	1.1
Gobi (Cabbage), grated	0.8
Bhindi (Ladies finger), chopped	0.8
Chawli leaves (Cow peas), chopped	0.7
Cauliflower leaves, chopped	0.5

All the nutritive values are calculated for 1 standard cup (200 ml.)
Please note that the weight per cup for each food will vary depending on its bulk density.